Army Aviation in Ulster

Guy Warner with Alex Boyd

Colourpoint

Nothing is impossible
Motto of 5 Regiment Army Air Corps

All rights reserved. No part of this publication may be reproduced, stored in a retrieval system or transmitted in any form or by any means, electronic, mechanical, photocopying, scanning, recording or otherwise, without the prior written permission of the copyright owners and publisher of this book.

6 5 4 3 2 1

© Guy Warner and Alex Boyd
2004

Designed by Colourpoint Books,
Newtownards
Printed by The Universities Press (Belfast) Ltd

ISBN 1 904242 27 8

Colourpoint Books
Colourpoint House
Jubilee Business Park
21 Jubilee Road
Newtownards
County Down
Northern Ireland
BT23 4YH
Tel: 028 9182 0505
Fax: 028 9182 1900
E-mail: info@colourpoint.co.uk
Web-site: www.colourpoint.co.uk

Guy Warner has been a regular contributor to *Ulster Airmail*, the journal of the Ulster Aviation Society, for eight years and has also written for *Aircraft Illustrated, Air Enthusiast, Air Pictorial, Aviation Ireland* and *Northern Ireland Travel News*. He is also co-author of Colourpoint's *In the Heart of the City: The History of Belfast's City Airport, 1938–1998, Flying from Malone: Belfast's First Civil Aerodrome* and *Belfast International Airport: Aviation at Aldergrove since 1938*. Guy is a teacher at Ben Madigan Preparatory School, is married with two daughters and lives in Co Antrim.

Alex Boyd is a keen amateur photographer and a chance introduction to the personnel of what is now 5 Regiment Army Air Corps has since given him many opportunities to photograph the machines they fly – Lynx and Gazelle helicopters and Islander fixed-wing aircraft – all in the Northern Ireland operating environment. Alex has provided many of the photographs from his own collection, as well as selecting others from various archives and private collections, and has written detailed captions for all. He is a retired draughtsman and married with a daughter.

Photo credits:

Front cover: An well-taken shot for the photographer as 655 Squadron Lynx XZ673 departs from the main helipad at Bessbrook on 15 September 1997.
KA Boyd

Rear cover: An unidentified DHC Beaver is pictured over Belfast city centre in the mid 1970s. The City Hall can be clearly seen (centre right) as can Oxford Street bus station and the Royal Courts of Justice (top left of the photograph).
Museum of Army Flying

Contents

Foreword by HRH The Prince of Wales......................5
Foreword by Brigadier RPD Folkes OBE, ADC...............6
Introduction..8
Acknowledgements.......................................11
In Memoriam...12

Part 1 Army aviation – a brief history from 1878.....13
  The Ulster connection...............................13
  From balloons and kites to dirigibles and heavier-than-air craft...18
  The spirit of the RFC...............................25
  To war..27
  Army co-operation...................................31
  The Army Air Corps in World War Two.................31
  Post-war and rebirth................................34

Part 2 Army aviation in Northern Ireland from 1957...41

Part 3 5 Regiment Army Air Corps....................75
  1 Flight..77
  655 Squadron..81
  665 Squadron..90
  5 Regt AAC Workshop REME............................98

Part 4 Flying with 5 Regiment......................102
  1 Flight...102
  655 Squadron.......................................105
  665 Squadron.......................................108

Corps and Squadron emblems............................111
Bibliography..112

His Royal Highness The Prince of Wales
Colonel-in-Chief of the Army Air Corps

CLARENCE HOUSE

There has been an association between Army aviation and Northern Ireland ever since Captain George Dawes landed his Maurice Farman Longhorn biplane on the beach at Newcastle, County Down, on 1st September 1913. It was not, however, until the early 1970's, with the start of the troubles in the Province, that the Army Air Corps started to play a leading military role.

During the past thirty years, their helicopters and small fixed-wing aircraft have been at the centre of operations and the pilots and aircrew have developed a justifiable reputation at the forefront of their professions.

As Colonel-in-Chief of the Army Air Corps, I have always been immensely proud of the gruelling and often dangerous work carried out by No.5 Regiment. The flying hours logged by aircrews supporting ground troops in Northern Ireland are simply staggering, and their contribution to operations has been out of all proportion to their number. Sadly, some have also paid the ultimate sacrifice in the service of their Regiment and their Country.

This book chronicles the contribution made by Army aviation in the Province and, in particular, the role of No.5 Regiment. As such, it will form an important historical record.

Foreword by Brigadier RPD Folkes OBE, ADC
Director Army Aviation

Army Air Corps aircrew have flown in many different countries and experienced the most wonderful combinations of landscapes and weather conditions, each providing a palette of colour, texture and light. But few places can compare with Northern Ireland and the watery dawn of a south Armagh morning, with the low mist shimmering in the valleys and the mountains of Mourne as a backdrop. Equally, flying below the tops of the majestic cliffs on the north coast of Co Antrim, which stand like a fortress against the incoming North Atlantic surf, is an exhilarating experience. Little did Captain Dawes of the Royal Flying Corps know when he landed on the beach in Newcastle, Co Down that a few generations later his successors in the army would spend over thirty years on continuous flying operations in the Province.

Northern Ireland for army aviators has been not only a wonderful country in which to fly but also a challenging operational theatre. it has been a popular posting because of the high flying rates and a special atmosphere – there has always been an operational 'buzz' about the place. Since mid 1969, Army Air Corps aircrew and groundcrew and the Royal Electrical and Mechanical Engineers maintainers have provided a round the clock capability, 365 days each year, in support of the security forces. They are recognised for their skill, professionalism and determination always to get the job done. Many an infantry patrol has been gratefully picked up in near impossible flying conditions, rejoicing at the familiar sound of the Scout or Lynx piercing the gloom as it groped its way towards them through the rain, wind and darkness.

It is this spirit of determination and grit that has been, and continues to be, the hallmark of the Army Air Corps and the way it conducts its operations. I am very grateful to Guy Warner for capturing this essence in his well-researched book on Army Aviation in Ulster. It is a story of service, bravery and sacrifice. As the first Commanding Officer to arrive in-post after the re-titling of 5 Regiment Army Air Corps, I had the opportunity to design a regimental badge. There was no question about the choice of motto for the regiment; the motto of our forebears in the Glider Pilot Regiment expresses the ethos of Army aviators and fits the bill for operations in Northern Ireland exactly – 'Nothing is impossible'.

Middle Wallop
June 2004

Sikorsky R6 Hoverfly 2 KN844 served with 1901 Flight in 1947 at Andover.

Flight International

The WAH-64 Apache Longbow AH1 is the most potent aircraft ever flown by the Army Air Corps.

Westland Helicopters Ltd

Introduction

The progress made by the Army Air Corps over the last 40 years or so has been quite remarkable. For the first decade or more of its existence it was derided as 'teeny-weeny airways', the poor relations in the world of military aviation when compared to the Royal Air Force and the Royal Navy. However, it is today a major combat arm of the British forces and is equipped with a very potent battlefield weapon, the WAH-64 Apache Longbow AH1 helicopter.

It can be argued that the conflict in Northern Ireland over the last thirty years has been the making of the AAC. It has performed a variety of operational tasks in often very difficult political and military circumstances. In all weathers and often with considerable hazard to the crews, the AAC has developed great skill, expertise and esprit de corps. In the words of the Duke of Wellington it has given the security forces the ability to "guess what was at the other side of the hill". Indeed, it is of interest that the guiding principle of army aviation when it made its debut in battle in 1914, was that reconnaissance was of prime importance. The first commander in the field of the Royal Flying Corps, Brigadier General Sir David Henderson, wrote the training manual *The Art of Reconnaissance* in 1907, before learning to fly in 1911 at the age of 49, in order to study and report on the practical applications of the aeroplane to this task. The following year another seminal figure learned to fly, Major Hugh Trenchard DSO of the Royal Scots Fusiliers. This account sets the work of today's army aviators in its historical context both in Northern Ireland and with regard to the development of army aviation since the final quarter of the 19th century.

I have found the sense of pride and purpose within 5 Regiment to be almost tangible. There is a distinct 'can do' atmosphere. The regimental motto 'Nothing is Impossible' is no idle or empty boast. I have found nothing but help, interest and the most friendly co-operation from all the personnel whom I have plagued with my questions. A list of all those interviewed or who otherwise gave of their time and effort, is appended below but it would only be fair to single out Major Penny Kitson AAC for special thanks; as the regimental liaison officer she dealt with all my enquiries with the greatest good humour and patience. I am also greatly indebted to Mr Keith Lloyd for permission to make use of his exhaustive and very detailed statistical survey of the AAC presence in Ulster from 1957. Thanks must also go to two commanding officers of 5 Regiment – Lieutenant Colonel Colin Baulf extended an always cheerful welcome and was a constant source of encouragement; the painstaking and invaluable proof reading carried out by Lieutenant Colonel Duncan Venn is also very much appreciated. I must also record thanks to the team at Colourpoint Books for turning the text and photographs into such a splendidly produced book. Finally, as ever, special thanks must go to my wife, Lynda, without whose support, coffee and biscuits this work would not have been possible.

I have been left with a feeling of immense admiration for all the men and women of the Corps. I hope that this account does them sufficient justice.

Others to whom thanks are due: Major General Sir Peter Downward, Brigadier Maurice Sutcliffe (formerly GPR), Brigadier Edward Tait AAC (retd), Colonel Derek Armitage RE (retd), Lieutenant Colonel Steve Welch AAC, Major RH Fitzgibbon REME (special thanks are due to Fitz for the research he very kindly undertook on my behalf at the REME Museum of Technology, Arborfield), Major George 'Smokey' Bacon AAC (an unparalleled source of ideas, enthusiasm and useful contacts), Major Alan Wiles AAC (retd), Major Alan Barbone AAC, Major James Ilingworth AAC, Captain 'Ginge' Smith AAC, Captain Martin Broomhead AAC, Captain Mark Martin AAC, Captain Steve Graham AAC, Captain CM Daly AAC, Captain Peter Wilson GPR, Captain Rob Phayre AAC, Captain Stuart Bourne AAC (who smoothed my way around 665 Squadron), Captain Steve Pengilly AAC, Lieutenant Matthew Aplin AAC, Lieutenant James Barr AAC, WO1 (ASM) Clive Mansley REME (who gave up several hours of his time to show me around the workshops), WO2 Kev Bridge AAC, WO2 Chris Sherlock AAC, WO2 Paul Bradbury AAC, WO2 AS Doidge Int Corps, Sergeant Martin Darlington AAC, Sergeant Gary Leigh AAC, Sergeant Dean Jobson AAC, Sergeant 'Jono' Johnson AAC, Sergeant Nick Parish AAC, Sergeant Jamie Thomsett AAC, Corporal Ed Brown RE, Airtrooper Dan Moran AAC, Airtrooper Adrian Monteith AAC, Mr Brian Graham, Mr Eric Myall, Mr Michael Clarke, Mr Stuart Leslie, Mr Peter Devitt, Mrs Patricia Murdock.

Guy Warner

The WAH-64 Apache is a derivative of the US Army's AH-64D Apache Longbow, the next generation of the combat proven AH-64A Apache. In addition to Rolls Royce engines the WAH-64 includes a number of systems unique to the UK.   *Westland Helicopters Ltd*

Through my initial meeting and subsequent involvement with photographing No 72 Squadron and their Wessex helicopters, I was eventually admitted to the helipad at Bessbrook and was thus introduced to their Mutual Support colleagues in the Northern Ireland Regiment, now 5 Regiment, Army Air Corps. My primary interest lay with trying to record the personnel and locations as well as the Lynx, Gazelle and, latterly, Islanders and I here acknowledge all those who assisted me in this respect.

Until asked by Lieutenant Colonel Baulf and Guy Warner to provide some of my own shots, select others from various archives and private collections and write the captions for a total of some 125 photographs, I had no idea of the extent and duration of army aviation in Ulster, certainly not from 1913, so this has proved to be an educational exercise as well as an enjoyable one. I regard this publication as a tribute to all the military personnel who have served in the Province during these and earlier 'troubles'. Guy's introduction has recorded many of those to whom thanks are due and to that list I would wish to add Corporal Paul Firth RAF of the RIGC(NI), whose invaluable assistance and technical expertise has made many of the earlier views useable and improved all of them, including my own!

My wife, Ruth, and daughter, Caroline's contribution to and toleration of the time spent on this project also deserves heartfelt acknowledgement.

The images range through early army fixed-wing aviation from the collections of Ernie Cromie, Stuart Leslie, AD (Donnie) Nelson, Brendan Treacy and Jack Woods to the Auster Mk 6s, personnel and Cessna 'Bird Dog' of 1913 Light Liaison Flight recorded by Captains PF Wilson and PA Downward. As well as shots of two Austers at RAF Aldergrove and a Saro Skeeter at RAF Bishopscourt c1960, Ray Burrows, of the Ulster Aviation Society, covered the Sioux, Scouts and Beavers at Sydenham and Aldergrove during the 1970s. These dated views may well prompt former aircrew from that era to check their log book entries.

Apart from the Omagh photographs of Sioux and Scout from 1976, my own material is of relatively recent origin. In this respect I would appreciate hearing from any personnel whose records match the dates and serials in the captions. This applies to the Ray Burrows views as well and all letters and e-mails sent to me, via the publisher, will be replied to.

I would also thank 40 Royal Marines Commando and Mirror Group Newspapers for permission to use the view of Scout XT638 leaving Bessbrook with an Eagle patrol during 1976. Does any reader know of the photographer or the whereabouts of the original photograph?

The reproduction of the Arnhem painting by Lynn Williams is reproduced courtesy of Airlife Publishing Ltd. Thanks, too, to David Brook, Editor of the Glider Pilot Regiment's *The Eagle* journal and to Alastair Taylor for permission to include the picture of the glider pilots featured on page 32.

A 1995 shot of 1 Flight Islander ZG844 at Ballykelly by RIR Major (now Lt Col) LJD Callow is included, together with an aerial view of the former RAF base from 655 Squadron's archive. During the same year an airship returned to army service with the trials of Westinghouse's Skyship 500; photos taken by Staff Sergeant DA Blackband and 5 Regiment's albums provided a record of its visit to Northern Ireland.

The Museum of Army Flying at Middle Wallop in Hampshire has an extensive photograph collection from the earliest days of army aviation. Thanks are due to Brigadier Edward Tait and Colonel Derek Armitage for their help in sourcing and providing material, both written and photographic, from both the Museum's archive and Brigadier Tait's personal records.

A further comparison is provided between the aircraft carrier images from 1957, supplied by Captain PF Wilson and the 655 Squadron Lynx practising deck landings on RFA *Fort George* in 2001. The Ulster Aviation Society was the source for a print of the now-preserved Grumman Wildcat being recovered from Portmore Lough (thanks to the sterling efforts of 655 Squadron), while Guy Warner recorded three of 665's Gazelles on the 'City Flight' tasking in July 2001. As with the 72 Squadron history, I trust that the photographic content, much of which is previously unpublished, will complement Guy's well-researched text to form an appropriate tribute to both the story of Army aviation in Ulster and 5 Regiment's current service in Northern Ireland.

Alex Boyd

Acknowledgements

Sincere thanks are due to the following, without whose sponsorship the publication of this work would not have been possible:

Carrickfergus Borough Council

Lady Mairi Bury Milibern Trust *Enkalon Foundation*

General Officer Commanding
(Northern Ireland) **Esme Mitchell Trust**

The Lord O'Neill Charitable Trust **5 Regiment Army Air Corps**

In Memoriam

There is a memorial in St Catherine's Church, Killead, Aldergrove which is inscribed in memory of those members of army aviation who died in the service of their country in Northern Ireland.

SSgt RE Hall DWR	8 July 1958	(Auster 6 – wirestrike)
Capt M Cracknell RA	13 November 1958	(Auster 6 – treestrike)
Capt RS Dove RVR	28 May 1960	(Accidental drowning)
Sgt DC Reid REME	24 June 1972	(Landmine – Glenshane Pass)
LCpl D Moon REME	24 June 1972	(Landmine – Glenshane Pass)
Pte C Stevenson PARA	24 June 1972	(Landmine – Glenshane Pass)
C/Sgt A Place PWO	18 May 1973	(Car bomb – Omagh)
CoH BR Cox RHG/D	18 May 1973	(Car bomb – Omagh)
Sgt DB Reid RM	18 May 1973	(Car bomb – Omagh)
Sgt S Young RMP	18 May 1973	(Car bomb – Omagh)
WO2 DC Rowat AAC	12 April 1974	(Scout crash near Lisburn)
Maj JD Hicks AAC	18 December 1975	(Sioux crash near Long Kesh)
WO2 BA Jackson AAC	7 January 1976	(Scout crash – South Armagh)
Cpl A Ford R Signals	7 January 1976	(Scout crash – South Armagh)
Capt MJ Kett RA	10 April 1978	(Scout crash – Lough Neagh)
Capt AJ Stirling AAC	2 December 1978	(Scout crash – Lough Ross)
Cpl RD Adcock PARA	2 December 1978	(Scout crash – Lough Ross)
Sgt KJ Robson RE	18 February 1980	(Gazelle crash near Lisburn)
Cpl RJ Jackson AAC	5 July 1980	(Traffic accident)
Sgt RT Gregory REME	22 October 1982	(Illness)
Cpl B McKenna REME	6 April 1982	(Illness)
LCpl SV Roberts REME	28 November 1984	(Traffic accident)
LCpl T Orange AAC	20 October 1987	(Accident)
Sgt JNP Croft AAC	14 August 1989	(Illness)
Cpl MD Ioannou REME	15 April 1995	(Traffic accident)
SSgt SJ Thompson REME	30 June 1995	(After surgery)

"They loved not their lives unto death."

2003 ended in tragic circumstances with the deaths of Captain Andrew Nicoll AAC and Sergeant Simon Bennett AAC in the crash of a Gazelle of 665 Squadron near Londonderry on 22 December, while on a flight from Omagh to Ballykelly. This book is dedicated to their memory and to all Army aviators who have given their lives in the service of the entire community in Northern Ireland.

Part 1: Army aviation – a brief history

The Ulster connection

The first association between army aviation and Ulster was truly historic. It occurred on 1 September 1913 at 1.50 pm when Captain George William Patrick Dawes landed on the beach at Newcastle, Co Down near the Slieve Donard Hotel. This was the first ever overseas deployment of the Royal Flying Corps (RFC). Five BE2a aircraft, serial numbers 217, 218, 272, 225 and 273, flown by Captains JWH Becke, CAH Longcroft and ACH McClean, Lieutenants FF Waldron and L Dawes respectively and a single Maurice Farman Longhorn, No 207, piloted by Captain GWP Dawes, all of No 2 Squadron based at Montrose, flew from Scotland on their way to take part in large-scale Irish Command manoeuvres centred around Rathbane Camp near Limerick.

Flotation bags had been fitted to the underside of the wings of the aircraft at Cults Farm on the Earl of Stair's estate near Castle Kennedy, as a precaution in case of ditching in the often choppy waters of the North Channel. These did nothing to improve the flying or handling qualities of the aeroplanes. Some degree of reassurance, though, was provided by the presence of the super-dreadnought HMS *Bellerophon*, cruising in the vicinity of the route. It may be noted that the warship's name was a happy chance in the light of its future association with soldiers of the air – Bellerophon being the rider of the winged horse Pegasus. (see page 76)

George Dawes, who was born in Dublin on 25 January 1881, had earned a battlefield commission in the South African War, with the Royal Berkshire Regiment

Maurice Farman 'Longhorn' No 207 of No 2 Squadron RFC is seen at Montrose during 1913; Capt GWP Dawes is in the cockpit.
AD Nelson collection

13

Army Aviation in Ulster

and was the first serving officer in the British Army to be awarded the Royal Aero Club Pilot's Certificate, flying a Humber Monoplane at Wolverhampton. He received Certificate No 17 on 26 July 1910 – AV Roe, the founder of the famous aero company, was No 18. In 1912 he joined the Military Wing of the Royal Flying Corps and was posted to No 2 Squadron at Farnborough. It is of interest to note that the first appearance of the RFC as a separate unit in the Army List was in October 1912. In February 1913 the squadron moved to Montrose.

It had been Dawes' task to travel by steamer to Larne, to scout out possible landing sites (it is possible that he flew over in the Maurice Farman S7 No 215 sometime in the last week of August 1913 but this cannot be confirmed). The local press reported that he had selected a field on Islandmagee, near Larne, as being ". . . suitable in every way for the brief occupation of the airmen." The town missed its chance to be part of this memorable event as ". . . the commercial instincts of the owner of the land obviated the acceptance of the officer's terms, which were said to have been fairly liberal." It was also noted in the *Larne Weekly Telegraph* that on Wednesday 27 August ". . . the observer of the Royal Army Aero Corps who had visited Islandmagee to select ground for the descent of the Army biplanes at present in Scotland paid a visit to Mr Hawker and proffered the assistance of mechanics, etc".

Officers of No 2 Squadron Royal Flying Corps (Military Wing), August 1913.

Left to right: Captain CAH Longcroft, Welch Regiment; Captain GWP Dawes, Royal Berkshire Regiment; Major JWH Becke; Lieutenant FF Waldron, 19th Hussars; Lieutenant ACH McClean; Captain F StG Tucker and Lieutenant L Dawes, Middlesex Regiment. Behind them is one of the Squadron's BE2a biplanes. All of these aviators – apart from Captain Tucker – flew to Ireland on 1 September 1913.

Army aviation – a brief history

A BE2a aircraft of No 2 Squadron RFC is seen taking off from Montrose in 1913 while, on the ground are a pair of S7 Longhorns (including No 215 mentioned opposite) and another BE2a.

JM Bruce/GS Leslie Collection

Another of No 2 Squadron's aircraft, BE2a No 273, is seen at Castle Kennedy before its flight to Ireland.

JM Bruce/GS Leslie Collection

Army Aviation in Ulster

Captain Dawes' Maurice Farman 'Longhorn' and three of the five BE2a biplanes of No 2 Squadron RFC at Cults Farm, Castle Kennedy in August 1913. The flotation bags for the North Channel crossing referred to in the text are clearly visible on No 272. Some years ago Mr Donnie Nelson, a reporter with a Stranraer newspaper, was given a first-hand account of this scene by an elderly gentleman from the town, Mr William McConnell. As a child, Willie McConnell helped mark out the field to be used, with two of his mother's white table-cloths. He lived in an adjacent cottage and may well be the boy in the photograph.

JM Bruce/GS Leslie Collection

This second view of Captain GWP Dawes in the cockpit of his Maurice Farman Longhorn, No 207, was taken at Castle Kennedy immediately prior to the flight to Ireland on 1 September 1913. The specially fitted flotation bags can be clearly seen under the wings.

AD Nelson collection

The great airman, Harry Hawker, had landed his Sopwith Hydro-Tractor Biplane seaplane on Larne Lough that morning, beating the Army's aviators by a few days as the first to make an aerial crossing to Ulster.

The Belfast newspaper, the *Northern Whig* reported Dawes' landing under the headline:

> Army Flying Corps – Captain Dawes alights at Newcastle – He passed over the sea to opposite the centre of the town, where he turned and flew towards the sandy part of the beach near the Slieve Donard Hotel and had a most graceful descent. Captain Magill received the intrepid airman and ministered to his wants and also assisted in overhauling the machine. After replenishing the petrol tank, Captain Dawes set the propeller in motion at 2.50 pm and swept along the beach for a short distance in the direction of Dundrum and rose. Turning, he proceeded with his mechanic, Mr Traylor, who arrived on 30th of the month to inspect the beach for the purpose of alighting. He flew in a southerly direction, skirting the Mourne Mountains, flying at a height of about 1000 feet. A very large crowd assembled on the beach and numerous camera operators were busily engaged photographing the airman and his machine. The other aircraft did not stop. They passed Newcastle at 1.45 pm, 3.32 pm and 3.45 pm, the last machine especially flying at a very high altitude.

The final aircraft was the BE2 piloted by Lieutenant Dawes. He broke his journey at the Royal Field Artillery Barracks in Dundalk and reported that he had maintained a height of 3000 feet. (The next day the *Belfast Evening Telegraph* featured photographs of Captain Dawes' aeroplane on the beach, with the crowd milling around, and one of his machine airborne.) The arrivals caused something of a sensation in Limerick that evening ". . . two of which had overflown the city before they steered for the camp at Rathbane, where a hearty reception was given to the aeronauts on their arrival by the troops and the constabulary in the camps and by the numbers of the public who walked, motored, and cycled there."

More than 20,000 troops were involved in the exercises, divided into the 'Brown Army' and the 'White Army'. A contemporary report from the 'battlefield' stated:

> During the early stages of the fight, the airmen of both sides were constantly in flight. The amount of information the observers in these machines were able to convey to their respective generals either directly or by means of messages dropped from the dizzy heights to units of the force was most valuable. All the while the machines went steadily, fortunately without any accident to their intrepid pilots and observers.

Rathbane is the location for this picture BE2a No 217, the aircraft flown by Captain JWH Becke.

Brendan Treacy collection

Some of No 2 Squadron's ground crew are pictured with their transport and stores at Rathbane in September 1913.
Brendan Treacy collection

After taking part in the exercises they returned home safely by the end of the month, having flown an average of 2000 miles each over the period. This was a very noteworthy feat for those early days; crossing the short stretch of sea between Scotland and Ireland, twice, in a rudimentary flying machine with a 70 hp engine and a top speed of between 50 and 70 mph was not a challenge for the faint-hearted. Moreover some very useful field experience had been gained. It was also a considerable technical achievement that there had been only one forced landing, Maurice Farman No 207 being extensively damaged at Ballyhornan on 24 September. It may indeed be regarded as a highly successful dress rehearsal for the operational deployment of the Royal Flying Corps to France just under a year later.

The aerial crossing to Ireland had only been accomplished five times previously, partially by Robert Loraine, who landed in the sea just off the coast in 1910, twice by Denys Corbett-Wilson in 1912, by Vivian Hewitt also in 1912 and by Harry Hawker in the Sopwith seaplane from Oban to Larne Harbour on 27 August 1913. Corbett-Wilson later served with No 3 Squadron; he was shot down and killed in 1915. Loraine also served with distinction in the RFC.

Captain Dawes later commanded No 11 Squadron on the Western Front in 1915. He rose to the rank of Colonel, ending the war in the Balkans as the Commanding Officer of the RAF forces there. He retired the following year with the rank of Wing Commander and served again in that rank for the duration of the Second World War. He died in 1960 at the age of 80. Captain Becke became a Group Captain before he retired in 1920, with the honorary rank of Brigadier General. Captain Longcroft, who had originally joined the Welch Regiment, attained the rank of Air Vice Marshal before he retired in 1929. All three were awarded the DSO. Lieutenant Waldron, who had first served as a cavalryman with the 19th Hussars, was a Major and commanding No 60 Squadron when he was shot down and killed over Cambrai on 3 July 1916. Lieutenant McClean rose to command Numbers 5 and 8 Squadrons and later became a Lieutenant Colonel and Commandant of the Central Flying School. Lieutenant Leonard Dawes, late of the Middlesex Regiment, who was not related to George, commanded No 29 Squadron on its formation as the third single-seater scout squadron equipped with DH 2s. It would be of interest for the author to learn of the regiments with which Becke and McClean started their military careers.

From balloons and kites to dirigibles and heavier-than-air craft

The origins of the exploitation of air power by the British Army extend back some 30 years previously to 24 June 1880, with the earliest recorded use of a balloon detachment on manoeuvres at Aldershot. Experiments with free and captive balloons had been carried out at Woolwich

Army aviation – a brief history

'Ballooning c1896.' Taken from the *AAC Journal*: 1957–1982.

Museum of Army Flying

The gentleman in the balloon basket is Major James Templer, Commander of the Balloon School, Farnborough; the unfortunate 'sapper' perched precariously above is unidentified.

Museum of Army Flying

Army Aviation in Ulster

The crew of an Army observation balloon in August 1911.

Museum of Army Flying

Arsenal in 1878 under the command of Captain RP Lee RE and Captain JLB Templer, 2nd Middlesex Militia. In fact from 23 August 1878 Templer was even granted 10 shillings (50p) a day flying pay for services as an instructor – though only on actual flying days. £150 was spent on the balloon, *Pioneer*, which took to the air that day. A "thoroughly sound and reliable fleet" of five balloons was established including *Sapper, Heron, Fly* and *Spy*, with a few officers and men trained to use them.

Balloon sections accompanied army expeditions to Bechuanaland in 1884 and the Sudan in 1885. A balloon establishment was put on paper in 1887, after which a permanent balloon section of the Royal Engineers was formed in May 1890, moving from Chatham to Aldershot in 1891. It was about this time that an early army aeronaut was reproved for being without helmet, sword, sabretache or spurs whilst on duty. The army also used balloons for observation and artillery spotting purposes in the Boer War between 1899 and 1902, notably at Magersfontein and in the siege and relief of Ladysmith. It was noted that aerial observation greatly increased the accuracy and effectiveness of artillery fire, much to the annoyance of the enemy. The balloon wagons were towed by teams of oxen in this campaign. By 1903 the Balloon Section had 150 officers and men and 36 horses. A further change of location was made in the winter of 1904/5 to a new site on Farnborough Common.

Balloons had proved their usefulness but they were

Army aviation – a brief history

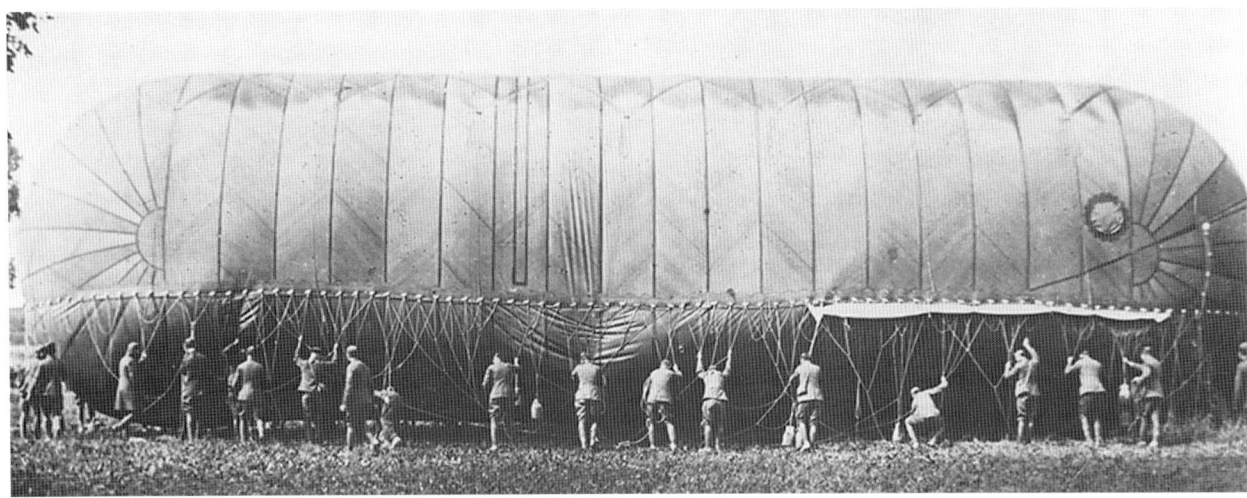

The ground crews are an important part of the Army flying team. Here we see a crew handling the Army's first airship, *Nulli Secundus*. Look at how many men are required to deal safely with this aircraft.

Museum of Army Flying

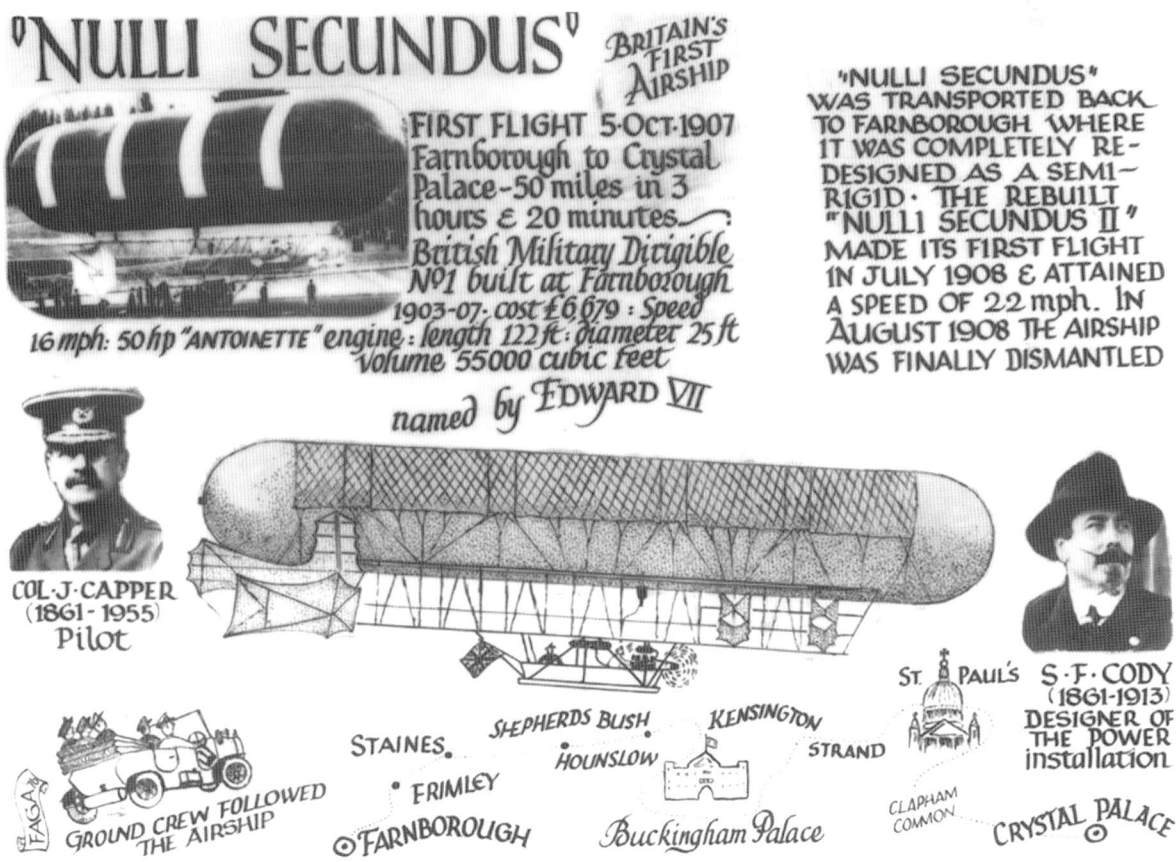

This card was produced to commemorate the first flight of *Nulli Secundus* from Farnborough to Crystal Palace on 5 October 1907.

Frederick G Foley/Museum of Army Flying

21

Army Aviation in Ulster

Major BFS Baden-Powell and SF Cody experimented with kites for observation and photography. A Cody man-lifting kite is seen in this view taken about 1899.

Colonel SF Cody with British Army Aeroplane No 1 which he designed and built.

Museum of Army Flying

British Army Aeroplane No 1 is seen in flight, probably in the latter months of 1908.

Museum of Army Flying

Military Boxkite No 134, rebuilt from Boxkite No 19, is pictured over-flying Brooklands in 1913.

Museum of Army Flying

either tethered or were taken wherever the wind blew them. Moreover, they were large, round targets for enemy guns. A balloon also took a long time to unpack, inflate, launch, recover, deflate and stow away on its wagon. This wagon was usually horse drawn, though motive power was sometimes provided by traction engines. The use of new technology also extended to communications, experiments in wireless telegraphy being conducted. In May 1908, Colonel JE Capper RE and Lieutenant CJ Ashton RE ascended in the free balloon *Pegasus* to a height of 8000 feet and received signals from a wireless station some 80 miles distant. The next stage was provide the ability to steer the craft and to give them motive power. The first flight in the all too brief career of British Army Dirigible No 1 *Nulli Secundus* was from the Army Balloon Factory at Farnborough on 10 September 1907. This was a sausage-shaped balloon covered with a net, with a gondola, which could hold three crewmen, suspended below from a light framework. It was powered by a 40 hp engine. On 5 October it was flown to London in three and a half hours by Capper and SF Cody, circling St Paul's Cathedral and landing at Crystal Palace.

Another aspect of early army aviation was the man-lifting kite. Major BFS Baden-Powell, Scots Guards, the brother of the founder of the Boy Scouts, developed a kite for reconnaissance and was the first to be taken aloft by this means on 27 June 1894. His kites were used during the Boer War for observation and photography. Later, the Texan, Samuel Franklin Cody, was employed by the War Office to experiment with observation kites on Woolwich Common and as a kite instructor in the Balloon Section of the Royal Engineers at Farnborough. If being in the wicker basket of a balloon felt vulnerable, then the prospect of dangling from a kite, a few hundred feet in the air, above a battlefield must have been a proposition for only the very brave or the most foolhardy.

On 16 October 1908, British Army Aeroplane No 1, piloted by the very same Samuel Cody, made its first short flight, also from Farnborough; this was the first officially recognised aeroplane flight in Great Britain. The aircraft was a single engine biplane of fragile aspect. Two pusher propellers were linked to the 50 hp Antoinette power unit by drive chains. The pilot sat with his back to the engine in a triangular canvas pram, manipulating a control wheel of the type normally associated with a tram.

Despite opposition from some in high quarters – "A useless and expensive fad, advocated by a few individuals whose ideas are unworthy of attention" asserted the Chief of the Imperial General Staff, General Sir WG Nicholson in 1910 – army aviation steadily began to make its mark. On 21 September 1910, Captain Bertram Dickson RFA demonstrated the flying capabilities of his Bristol Boxkite during army manoeuvres on Salisbury Plain. Five days later a wireless transmission was made from the air to the ground, using another Boxkite. Support was forthcoming

Military airship *Beta,* seen at Alderbury, Hants on 20 September 1910, seems to have generated much interest amongst the locals.
Museum of Army Flying

HM Airship *Gamma.*

Museum of Army Flying

from a senior officer – General Sir John French spoke with Captain Dickson expressing not only his own interest in the possibilities afforded by aviation in the field of reconnaissance but also remarking that all far-sighted military authorities should take a similar view.

On 1 April 1911, the Air Battalion of the Royal Engineers was formed – "... a body of expert airmen, organised in such a way as to facilitate the formation of units ready to take the field with troops and capable of expansion by reserve formations." In command was Major Sir Alexander Bannerman RE. It consisted of two companies, No 1 (Airship) at South Farnborough, commanded by Captain EM Maitland, Essex Regiment, and No 2 (Aeroplane) at Larkhill, under the command of Captain JDB Fulton RFA. Volunteer pilots had to learn to fly at their own expense and, if successful, were reimbursed £75 by the Government. One officer, Lieutenant RA Cammell RE, even brought his own aircraft, a Bleriot XXI monoplane, which was used in early wireless experiments. The Air Battalion was superseded by the formation, on 13 May 1912, of the Royal Flying Corps (RFC), which consisted initially of a Military Wing of one airship and man-carrying kite squadron and two aeroplane squadrons, a Naval Wing, a Central Flying School at Upavon in Wiltshire and the Royal Aircraft Factory at Farnborough. On 4 June 1912 Corporal Frank Rudd became the first NCO to gain a Royal Aero Club 'ticket', as the flying certificate was commonly known.

Aircraft undertook valuable liaison and reconnaissance functions during the annual manoeuvres of autumn 1912, in spite of the expressed opinion of Lieutenant General Douglas Haig that "flying can never be of any use to the Army." (To be fair, it should be noted that he subsequently changed his mind when he saw the value of the aircraft in battlefield conditions in the Great War.) General JM Grierson, commanding the Red forces, was heard to remark "Aircraft completely spoilt the war." The airships *Beta, Delta, Gamma* and *Eta* also performed usefully on manoeuvres and with experimental research into meteorology, aerial observation, parachuting and wireless telegraphy. On 1 July 1914, the Royal Naval Air Service (RNAS) took over responsibility for airships from the RFC.

The spirit of the RFC

In his book, *Five Years in the RFC*, the great air ace and former Royal Engineer, Major James McCudden VC, described the old prewar Flying Corps:

> The RFC at this time was roughly 800 NCOs and men strong with about 40 pilots. Despite, or perhaps owing to, its lack of numbers, it was very efficient and highly disciplined. This was due to the fact that the original NCOs of the RFC were largely transfers from the Guards, the Adjutant, Lieutenant Barrington-Kennett, being a Grenadier Guardsman. The Royal Engineers had also contributed largely to the personnel. What accounted for this excellent state of affairs was that the RFC tried to live up to Lieutenant Barrington-Kennett's vow that it should combine the smartness of the Guards with the efficiency of the Sappers. This was actually true of the prewar RFC.

A Maurice Farman Shorthorn pusher biplane is pictured with RFC personnel at an unknown location.
JM Bruce/GS Leslie collection

Army Aviation in Ulster

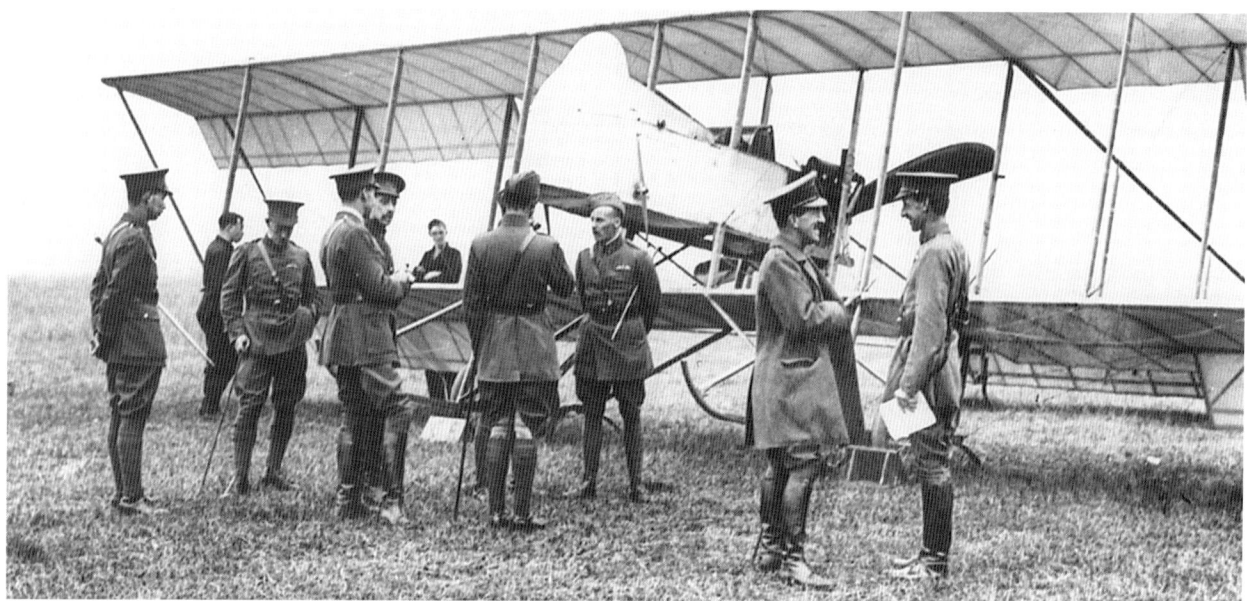

Maj Gen W Sefton Brancker (second right) is seen in conversation with Major F Sykes, the RFC's commander, and some of the first RFC personnel 'drawn from more than forty different regiments', in front of a Maurice Farman 'Shorthorn' biplane at Netheravon about 1913. On the outbreak of war he was appointed Deputy Director of Military Aeronautics and in later years, as Sir Sefton Brancker, went on to become a seminal force in British aviation before his untimely death in the 1930 R101 disaster.

JM Bruce/GS Leslie collection

As mentioned on page 29 Union Flags were painted on aircraft wings and tailfins to aid identification. This rare view of an RFC BE2a aircraft shows the Union flag on the tail.

JM Bruce/GS Leslie collection

Not quite a perfect landing! The Union flag identification was also painted on the underside of aircraft wings as can be seen on this BE2a aircraft.   *JM Bruce/GS Leslie collection*

To war

The attitude of the General Staff towards the aeroplane could still not be described as overwhelmingly enthusiastic, with the result that it was a very mixed bag of aircraft that assembled in a field at Swingate Downs, near Dover, to go to war some two years later. In mid-August 1914, 37 Avros, BE2s, BE8s, Bleriots and Farmans prepared to fly to France as the air component of the British Expeditionary Force (BEF), the largest mass flight in history to that date. The personnel were drawn from more than 40 different regiments. By way of mission equipment, each pilot and observer had been given a revolver, field glasses, a spare pair of goggles, a small stove, biscuits, cold meat, chocolate, soup cubes and strict instructions that nothing else should be carried. The previous day a transport column of 95 assorted army lorries, motor cars and requisitioned commercial vehicles had gone ahead by cross-channel ferry. Such was the requirement for aircraft that three Bleriot monoplanes belonging to 2nd Lieutenant Bucks were pressed into service, with the former owner being allocated one of his own machines, now numbered 619. The first to land in France was an Irishman, Lieutenant HD Harvey-Kelly of No 2 Squadron, flying BE2a No 347. (For his pains, he received a severe telling off from his squadron commander, Major JC Burke, who had also come from the Royal Irish Regiment, for having the temerity to arrive before his CO. Sadly Harvey-Kelly was one of the many who did not survive the war, being killed in 1917, when a Major commanding No 19 Squadron). The first war patrol, a reconnaissance mission, was flown a few days later, on 19 August, looking for enemy troops to the west of Brussels. The pilots were Captain PB Joubert de la Ferte RA, flying a Bleriot and Lieutenant GW Mapplebeck, Liverpool Regiment, in a BE2a.

Field Marshal Sir John French, the commander of the BEF, issued helpful instructions to soldiery who had the misfortune to find themselves in the path of an aeroplane wishing to land:

> An aeroplane requires an open and clear landing space and alights in the direct line in which it is travelling. The general rules for safety to be observed by troops in the presence of aircraft flying low are as follows:
> (a) Individuals or scattered parties will at once proceed to some fixed object, such as a tree or house.
> (b) Formed bodies of troops will halt, if possible, not in the direct line of flight.
> (c) Troops will not scatter in the open, as this makes any decision on the part of the pilot impossible.
> (d) Should it appear inevitable that an aeroplane flying low must strike any individuals, they should lie down in order to avoid being struck by the propeller.
> (e) When an aeroplane descends in the vicinity of troops, the commander of the latter will take steps to keep spectators clear of the ground upon which it is to alight.

He also added some kind words concerning the early achievements of the airmen and their craft:

> Their skill, energy and perseverance have been beyond

Army Aviation in Ulster

This RE8 of 105 Squadron RAF is seen over Omagh, Co Tyrone in 1918.

JM Bruce/GS Leslie collection

This aerial view of 105 Squadron's 'aerodrome' at Strathroy, on the northwest outskirts of Omagh, Co Tyrone, was taken in 1918.

E Cromie collection

all praise. They have furnished me with the most complete and accurate information, which has been of incalculable value in the conduct of operations. Fired at constantly, both by friend and foe and not hesitating to fly in every kind of weather, they have remained undaunted throughout.

The pilots had some rather less kind words for the enthusiastic troops, who in the early days tended to blaze away at anything flying overhead, regardless of its nationality. Many years later, the then Air Marshal Sir Philip Joubert recalled "To this day I can remember the roar of musketry that greeted two of our machines as they left the aerodrome and crossed the main Maubeuge–Mons road, along which a British column was proceeding." Henceforth, Union flags, painted on the undersides of machines, reduced but did not entirely eliminate the danger. From May 1915, the familiar, and distinctive, red, white and blue roundels and vertical stripes on the rudder were painted on British aircraft.

The proud and glorious history of the RFC does not form part of this account, save to say that under the inspirational leadership of Brigadier General Hugh Trenchard the offensive spirit that animated it was encouraged and developed. The guiding principle of the RFC was that it should never be found wanting in its commitment to support the army to the utmost, always remembering the awful conditions suffered by their fellow soldiers in the trenches. By 31 March 1918, the day before its absorption into the Royal Air Force, the Flying Corps had grown in size to 136 active squadrons, in the United Kingdom, France, Belgium, Italy, Macedonia, Mespotamia, Palestine, Egypt, Russia, South Africa and India. It had developed wide-ranging skills, which included aerial combat, reconnaissance both in a strategic sense and of the battlefield, artillery observation, air photography, ground attack, bombing and supply dropping.

A further early connection with Ulster should be noted here. In May 1918, No 105 Squadron, which was equipped with RE8s, was sent to Omagh. Its duties were to support the army on the ground on reconnaissance and communications tasks. The aim, in the words of the Lord Lieutenant of Ireland, Field Marshal Viscount French, was to ". . . put the fear of God into these playful Sinn Feiners."

During the inter-war period army officers were seconded to RAF Army Co-operation squadrons, which were equipped with aircraft such as the Hawker Hector (pictured above) and the Westland Lysander (see page 30). *Westland Helicopters Ltd*

Army Aviation in Ulster

A Westland Lysander of No 231 Squadron is seen on message pick-up duties at Newtownards on 11 May 1941.

E Cromie collection

Top notch facilities for aircraft maintenance weren't always available. When Auster TW445 required an engine change in north Africa, sometime in 1944, it had to be carried out in the field with only the most basic equipment available.

Museum of Army Flying

Army co-operation

In 1918 the RFC had achieved the status of an independent service with the creation of the RAF. However, this did not result in the complete abandonment of flying by the army, despite a less-than-ringing endorsement from Earl Haig in 1926 – "There will be a place for the tank and the aeroplane in future war but they will never replace the horse, the well-bred horse." During the inter-war period army officers were seconded to RAF Army Co-operation squadrons, which were equipped successively with types such as the Bristol Fighter, Armstrong Whitworth Atlas, Hawker Audax, Hawker Hector and Westland Lysander. Trials were also conducted with early rotary-wing types, the Cierva autogiros. About half the squadron pilots, including sometimes the commanding officer, were army officers. During World War Two some Army Co-operation flights and squadrons were based in Northern Ireland. Examples of these included the following: No 231 Squadron flew Lysanders at Newtownards in 1940/41 before transferring to Long Kesh and adding Curtiss Tomahawks, further moves being made to Maghaberry and Nutts Corner later in the war, and No 1494 Flight, also with Lysanders, was based at Long Kesh and then Sydenham. To these should be added the RAF's sixteen Air Observation Post (AOP) squadrons, in which most of the pilots were Royal Artillery officers and who flew Auster light aircraft on battlefield reconnaissance tasks. It is of interest to note the AOP squadrons were employed on tasks very similar to those carried out by the BE2s, RE8s and FK8s of the RFC's 'Corps Squadrons' during the Great War.

The initial trials were conducted in 1939 and resulted in the formation of a 'Flying Observation Post' unit, 'D' Flight at Old Sarum in Wiltshire, on 1 February 1940. It formed part of No 1 School of Army Co-operation within 22 Army Co-operation Group RAF. Inspiration and leadership was provided by Lieutenant Colonel Charles Bazeley DSO. The equipment was a motley assortment of impressed and requisitioned light aircraft – Taylorcraft, Stinsons and Piper Cubs. 'D' Flight deployed to France in April 1940 and swiftly redeployed back to Old Sarum a month later. The Air Ministry was most unenthusiastic but not for the first, or last, time, General Sir Alan Brooke exercised his considerable intelligence and authority. He stated that the army regarded AOP units as essential for the land campaigns which must take place in the future. So, on 1 August 1941, 'D' Flight became No 651 (AOP) squadron, with first Taylorcraft and then its British version, the Auster. The four Taylorcraft Plus C.2 of 'A' Flight No 651 Squadron were based in Ulster, briefly, in 1942, at Long Kesh.

The AOP squadrons saw action in North Africa, Sicily, Italy, northwest Europe and the Far East (mainly Burma). Relying on slow speed and manoeuvrability to evade enemy aircraft, AOP flights and squadrons operated in small numbers from any suitable field in close proximity to the ground forces with which they were operating. Perhaps the most remarkable feat of flying by an AOP pilot was in North Africa. His Auster was attacked by a Messerschmitt Bf 109, which was something of a one-sided contest. The Army pilot escaped almost certain destruction by descending into and flying around the crater of an extinct volcano until the German fighter got tired of waiting for him to emerge. The Auster returned home safely.

In 1946 Field Marshal Montgomery accorded them this accolade "The Air AOP . . . has become a necessary part of gunnery and a good aeroplane is required for the job. Very good RA officers are required for duty in the squadrons. It is not difficult to teach them to fly."

The Army Air Corps in World War Two

While today's Army Air Corps (AAC) takes pride in the achievements of these early progenitors, it traces its direct antecedents back to the Army Air Corps established early in the Second World War by Winston Churchill. This consisted of the Parachute Regiment, the Glider Pilot Regiment and the nucleus of what would later become the Special Air Service.

The Glider Pilot Regiment was formed in February 1942, under the command of Lieutenant Colonel John Rock. Following his untimely death in a training accident, Rock was succeeded by his second-in-command Major George Chatterton. The glider pilots and their Horsa, Hamilcar or Waco (Hadrian) gliders served with great distinction, taking part in airborne assaults in Sicily, Normandy, Southern France, Holland and Germany, as

Army Aviation in Ulster

Three pilots and a Horsa in 1943. Taken from the *Eagle* journal, this records Sgts Stewart Grey (left) and Alistair Taylor (centre). Can anyone identify the third pilot?

A Taylor/The Eagle *Journal*

This painting, 'The Arnhem Landing Zone', was produced by Lynn Williams for the jacket of *Silent Invader*, by Alexander Morrison, and later featured on the cover of the April 2000 *Eagle*.

L Williams / Airlife Publishing Ltd

A Horsa glider, being towed behind a Halifax tug, is pictured heading off on a mission.

Museum of Army Flying

well as operations with the Maquis and a supply mission to Tito's partisans in Yugoslavia.

Northern Ireland made a contribution in respect of the gliders. During the summer of 1942 long-distance training exercises were flown with Horsas, and small Hotspur training gliders, to Long Kesh and Nutts Corner.

The Airspeed Horsa has been described as a "massive exercise in carpentry", being 67 feet long, with a wingspan of 88 feet, made almost entirely of wood. The General Aircraft Hamilcar was even larger and could take a load of up to 7.8 tons. The Waco CG-4A, known as the Hadrian in British service, was the smallest, with a capacity for 14 troops.

The very special skills of the glider pilots were well summarised by General Sir Anthony Farrar-Hockley:

> It did not lie in the phase of taking off successfully a loaded glider in a high wind or in following a tug on a course (although these involved considerable skill). It lay in those minutes after casting off at night, over alien territory, poorly illuminated, if lit at all, when the pilots assumed the huge burden of finding their way down to a precise patch of ground, a few hundred square yards surrounded by obstacles any one of which might shatter the ply and canvas fuselage in a fatal collision.

Lieutenant General 'Boy' Browning very aptly described them as "total soldiers", they could fly and they could fight, they were truly an elite formation. A story is told of a glider crashing through a dyke, ripping off the undercarriage and most of the Horsa's floor. The pilot shouted to the troops in the rear, "Keep in step lads and we'll complete a good landing." In contrast to this humorous tale, another glider pilot told of flying through a storm of flak to effect a good landing, unharmed and protected by his armoured seat. He looked round and discovered his 29 passengers had not been so fortunate – they were all dead. Some 550 members of the regiment were killed on operations between 1942 and 1945.

The courage of the aviators of the Glider Pilot Regiment and the AOP Squadrons is staggering; flying slow, fragile, unarmed aircraft in the midst of battle takes a very special kind of bravery.

Army Aviation in Ulster

Normandy, 1944 and a Royal Tank Regiment officer is pictured briefing a 655 Squadron pilot prior to a reconnaissance flight.
Museum of Army Flying

Post-war and rebirth

The original AAC was disbanded soon after the war but four regular and five auxiliary AOP squadrons were retained for the observation role, photographic reconnaissance and light liaison/communications.

Service rotary-wing flying had begun in the 1930s with autogyros and had made the first steps with helicopters towards the end of the war. The Army was allocated three Sikorsky R-6s in 1947 and these were flown by Captains AC Gow, PRD Wilson and R Smith, of 1901 Flight, on trials and development work until April 1951. It had been retitled 1906 Flight in 1950 and it was under this name that it received four Bristol Sycamores in September 1951. For the next six years these aircraft were operated by army pilots, chiefly on VIP transport duties, role demonstrations and providing reconnaissance and mobility facilities for commanders at Army exercises. The first Saunders Roe Skeeters were delivered to the unit early in 1957 – nearly a decade after the maiden flight of the prototype W14 Skeeter 1 (G-AJCJ) on 8 October 1948. Not everyone was convinced of the battlefield utility of rotary-wing aviation; in 1954 the RAF Staff College was of the view that the helicopter would never be a "vehicle of war."

Another important contribution was made to the revival of army aviation in 1955 with the establishment of the Joint Experimental Helicopter Unit (JEHU) at Middle Wallop. Its purpose was to study the use of utility helicopters in the battle zone. It was equipped with six Sycamore HC14s and six Westland Whirlwind HAR2s. The CO was Lieutenant Colonel JFT Scott and his Second-in-Command was Squadron Leader DCL Kearns. Although manned jointly with the RAF, the whole cost of the unit was met from army funds and the aircraft were the first owned by the army since the days of the RFC. Trials work was considerably interrupted by JEHU's participation in the Suez campaign of 1956, airlifting the men of 45 Commando to Port Said from the deck of HMS *Ocean* – the first occasion in military history in which helicopters had been used in a full-scale assault. JEHU also has a connection with Ulster as, just before its disbandment in December 1959, it took part in Exercise Winged Coachman in the province. The aircraft carried out troop lifts and re-supply for 19 Infantry Brigade, in often adverse weather conditions, which in one 24-hour period alone included frost, snow, fog and rain. When a Sycamore landed on a hill top, the surface was so boggy that its undercarriage wheels were nearly submerged by the time the recovery party was flown in. All in all it was a useful demonstration of the helicopter's potential in Ulster. JEHU's aircraft were taken over by No 38 Group RAF.

On 1 September 1957 a nucleus of pilots from the Glider Pilot Regiment (which had been disbanded) was merged with the Air Observation squadrons to form the present day Army Air Corps.

From September 1958 the Royal Electrical and Mechanical Engineers (REME) assumed full responsibility for first and second line servicing and maintenance, tasks previously performed by RAF technicians. Some notion of the lean manning of REME may be gained from the fact that at the first meeting at the Air Ministry to discuss the details of the handover, 13 RAF engineers attended to face a solitary representative of REME. Indeed the fact that there were but three basic aircraft trades – later reduced to two – as compared to five trades in the RN and no less than seven in the RAF, has always been a source of considerable quiet,

Army aviation – a brief history

One of the Bristol Sycamore HC14s operated by JEHU from 1955 to 1959 is seen taking part in an exercise, while below a JEHU Westland Whirlwind HAR2 is demonstrating the helicopter's potential in recovering disabled aircraft.

Westland Helicopters Ltd

Army Aviation in Ulster

Above: Bristow's operated several Westland-built Augusta Bell 47G-4s for initial training of Army Air Corps pilots – an early example of public-private partnership, perhaps?
Below: A Westland Scout is seen in action in Aden.
both Westland Helicopters Ltd

understated satisfaction to REME. It was regarded as a good example of the versatility of the soldier when compared to his light and dark blue opposite numbers.

The permanent cadre of the Air Corps in the early years was small, comprising only about 80 officers and NCOs. The majority of pilots were regimental officers and senior NCOs seconded from their regiments on three-year flying tours. The administration of the Army Air Corps Centre at Middle Wallop was in the hands of the Royal Armoured Corps. In 1962 the first air troop was established within an armoured regiment. Though not necessarily the most financially efficient means of organisation, the air troops and air platoons helped create a sense of comradeship and a close bond with the parent regiment. Each flying unit was provided with a small team of REME technicians, often commanded by a Staff Sergeant. On the other hand, unless the parent formation

A Westland Lynx AH7 is seen on exercise 'somewhere in Germany'; it is kitted out for the anti-tank role.

Westland Helicopters Ltd

For 1987's *AAC Journal*, SSgt S Andrew put seven past and present types in formation near Middle Wallop.

SSgt S Andrew

was particularly air-minded, the aircraft tended to be misused and their maintenance suffered.

During the 1960s new aircraft were introduced – the Sioux AH1, Alouette II and Scout AH1 helicopters, as well as the principal fixed-wing type, the redoubtable Beaver AL1. In 1969, the RAF formally relinquished hold of the block of squadron numbers 650–670. The next great watershed was in 1972, when the Corps was enabled to recruit air troopers directly and to woo promising cadets at Sandhurst. No longer would it have to be mainly dependent on seconded personnel from other arms. A full career and good promotion prospects were available within the Corps. Moreover, the concept of operating as organic squadrons, rather than as air troops attached to other units, was being developed. REME first line support for each squadron was reorganised in the form of a Light Aid Detachment (LAD), commanded by a captain.

The basic concept of the rotary-wing element of the AAC was established as "The application of force by helicopter on the orders of a ground force commander." The hardware may have become considerably more effective and sophisticated over the years but original premise remains true to this day.

An opportunity to acquire an attack helicopter was missed in the 1970s with the cancellation of the Wildcat, which would have been based on the dynamics of the Lynx. Moreover, a staff requirement for two helicopters comparable to the American UH-1 and Chinook was dropped. New helicopters were introduced, however – the Gazelle AH1, in 1974 and the Lynx AH1, in 1977, of which 187 and 113 were ordered respectively. Both of these have given magnificent service in Northern Ireland. In the following decade another Army requirement which was cancelled was for a light transport or utility type – either the Westland WG30 or Westland/Sikorsky Blackhawk.

Close liaison and co-operation between those in the air, whether in helicopters or fixed-wing aircraft and on the ground is vital. The Corps prides itself on the fact that the crews of AAC aircraft are soldiers themselves and understand the problems and needs of the units over which they operate. The men of the Glider Pilot Regiment and the bulk of the AOP pilots were proud of being soldiers first and airmen second; the men and women of today's AAC deem this quality as being of no less importance. The AAC Guidon, which was presented to the Corps in 1994, is emblazoned not only with the battle honours gained in the Falkland Islands in 1982 and the Gulf War in 1991 but also with the badges of the Glider Pilot Regiment and of the Royal Artillery. (A Guidon is an heraldic banner carried by cavalry regiments and is the equivalent of the colours borne by regiments of line infantry.) Today the AAC consists of over 3200 personnel and operates in excess of 300 aircraft, principally the Gazelle and Lynx, with smaller numbers of the Islander, Agusta A.109 and Bell 212. Now entering service is the WAH-64 Apache Longbow AH1 attack helicopter, the most potent aircraft ever flown by the AAC.

Army aviation – a brief history

The Gazelle AH Mk 1 Light observation and communication helicopter (top) has been in service with the Army Air Corps since 1974. Manufactured by Westland as part of Anglo-French collaboration, which included Puma and Lynx, a total of 262 Gazelles were produced for the Army, Navy and Royal Air Force. One hundred and thirteen Lynx AH1s were supplied to the Army Air Corps. The Mk 7 (illustrated lower) was specifically configured to improve performance in the hover for long periods. Work began on converting existing Mk 1s to this standard in 1987.

Westland Helicopters Ltd

39

Auster AOP6 VF552 is seen at RAF Aldergrove about 1960. Note that the aircraft is secured to two large concrete blocks!

R Burrows

Group photograph of 1913 Squadron Light Liaison Flight. Seated l–r: Sgt Killilea; SSgt Hall; Sgt Meaton; Capt Baldwick; Capt PF Wilson; SSgt Ogsden; RAF Sgt ? ; Sgt Davies and SQMS Bezzum. July 1957.

Capt PF Wilson

Part 2: Army aviation in Northern Ireland

There has been a connection between Northern Ireland and the post-war AAC from the time of its inception.

On 14 February 1957 new aircraft arrived at RAF Aldergrove, in the shape of the five Auster Mk 6s of 1913 Light Liaison Flight – VF552, VF571, VF628, VF661 and WJ407. To begin with, the flight had been under the control of the RAF, though the pilots were all members of the Glider Pilot Regiment. The OC was Captain Peter Wilson. The other pilots were Captain Baldwick, Lieutenant Legg, Staff Sergeants Hall and Ogsden and Sergeants Meaton and Davies. They soon became 13 Flight, 651 Squadron, of the newly revived Army Air Corps (AAC) and in the words of the last CO of the GPR, Maurice Sutcliffe, "In September 1957 all the pilots simply transferred to the new Corps; we changed the red for the light blue and carried on."

1913 Flight had been formed in June 1951, commanded by Captain Peter Downward and shortly afterwards embarked for the Far East, for Korean War duties which lasted until 1955. It was equipped with Auster AOP6s, to which was added a US Army Cessna L–19A 14754, reportedly as a result of the Corps Commander, Lieutenant General 'Iron Mike' O'Danniel's, ". . . concern at the discomfort the GOC, Major General 'Jim' Cassels, suffered when travelling about in an Auster." The GOC had just had an unfortunate upside down landing in an Auster flown by his Canadian ADC. It was rumoured that the deal was sealed with a case of Scotch. The L19 'Bird Dog' was improved by the addition of RAF roundels and red plates with two stars attached on both sides of the engine

1913 Light Liaison Flight RAF (Army & RAF personnel) at Middle Wallop in August 1951, shortly before departure for Korea. At present only those in the front row have been identified as follows. L–R: LCpl ? (Army); Cpl Troy (RAF); Sgt Killilea (Army); Sgt Jermy (GPR); SSgt Hall (GPR); Capt Downward (OC 1913 Flt); Maj. Oldman (OC 657 Sqn); Maj King-Clark (OC GPR); Capt Brown (GPR); SSgt Thrippleton (GPR); Sgt Wright (GPR); Sgt Carr (RAF i/c A/c Servicing); Cpl Kirk (RAF); Cpl Knott (RAF).

Maj Gen PA Downward

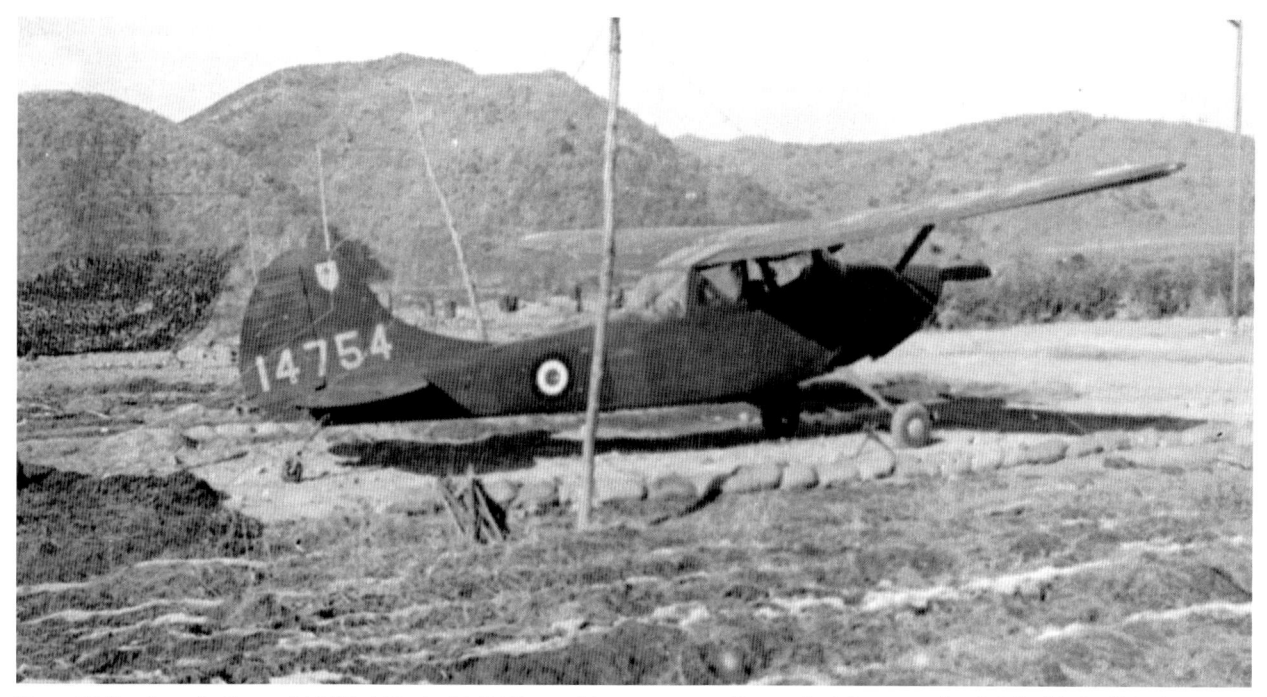

'Army 754' – the only Cessna L19 'Bird Dog' with RAF roundels – was reputedly acquired for use as the GOC's 'Air Staff Car' in Korea 1951, in a deal sealed with a case of Scotch. This caused great difficulty later with the accountants!   *Maj Gen PA Downward*

cowling. Captain Tony Brown was appointed the chauffeur of GOC's 'staff car'. Peter Downward later commented "Army 754 was truly a very comfortable kite to fly in and handled beautifully." However, for a number of years afterwards he was pursued by MOD accountants as, due to the unorthodox nature of the transaction, the correct paperwork could not be found to retire an aircraft which had never actually been formally part of Her Majesty's forces. By the time the conflict ended in 1953, the Flight had flown nearly 9000 sorties; it remained in Korea until 1955, when it returned to the UK.

The Flight's next operational commitment was in Cyprus and Egypt during the Suez Crisis of 1956. Back home at Andover, living up to its reputation for acquiring nonstandard aircraft, it 'borrowed' a Chipmunk T.10, WK549, which it managed to retain when it was posted to Northern Ireland.

The normal duties of 13 Flight included liaison flying and border patrols. Their contribution was valued greatly by the RUC and also by 39 Brigade. This period was the time of the IRA's 'Border Campaign' of 1956–62. The main airfields used, apart from Aldergrove, were RAF Ballykelly, RNAS Eglinton and St Angelo, Enniskillen, though a local agreement was also made to use a field near the beach at Tyrella, Co Down.

Peter Wilson particularly remembers an episode in November 1957, which was anything but routine:

> The Canadian aircraft carrier HMCS Bonaventure (which had been built in Belfast) had arrived in the port for a courtesy visit. A party was organised at Aldergrove for the Canadian officers. I was invited by the Commander Flying to land the Flight on the carrier. After a few G and Ts this seemed like a good idea, so I accepted. On the appointed morning, a signal from the ship informed us that she would be sailing five nautical miles south of Ailsa Craig (also known as Paddy's Milestone). The weather was clear and we planned to fly in loose formation at 5000 feet. After some forty minutes the rock loomed into view. I could also see what appeared to be a small fishing boat but Staff Sergeant Hall's voice came over the R-T "That's it below us now." It looked far too small to be the carrier and certainly much too small to consider landing on. However, as we descended it became reassuringly larger. I prepared to set a good example and make the first landing. Bonaventure was steaming obligingly into wind and all I had to do was to catch up and so make my first ever deck landing.

Army aviation in Northern Ireland

Group photograph at RAF Aldergrove. L–R: Lt Gen Sir Brian Kimmins; Lt Gen ? ; Gp Capt Burwell (Stn Cdr RAF Aldergrove); Capt PF Wilson (OC 13 Flt); Wg Cdr Plowright (Wg Cdr Flying, RAF Aldergrove).

Capt PF Wilson

Auster Mk 6 WE551 – pilot Capt PF Wilson DFC – lands on the Canadian aircraft carrier HMCS *Bonaventure* south of Ailsa Craig, off the Ayrshire coast, on 4 November 1947.

Capt PF Wilson

43

Three Auster Mk 6 aircraft of 13 Flight are picketed down on the deck of HMCS *Bonaventure* during their visit on 4 November 1957.
Capt PF Wilson

As I approached, various signals were coming from the ship but other than the green 'clear to land' light, the rest of the semaphore messages were unintelligible. With full flap down and 30 feet above the deck, turbulence made the aircraft almost uncontrollable. As I made contact with the deck, the port tyre burst on one of the wire hawsers that were so thoughtfully stretched across it at right angles – presumably in the hope that the Auster's tailhook (which due to an understandable oversight in design – as it was not intended to land on carriers – it did not possess) would catch onto one of them and so arrest further forward movement. Needless to say, we did not stop and slithered to port across the flightdeck. My passenger, Captain Neil Baldwick, decided that it was time to go and made the quickest exit from the aircraft that I have ever witnessed. He need not have bothered, however, as I managed to brake before the aircraft reached the side of the ship, while a couple of matelots grabbed the struts. The rest of the Flight, having observed my pioneering efforts carefully, all landed safely. While we were enjoying refreshments in the wardroom, my port wheel inner tube was replaced by an equivalent part from a Canadian helicopter. All too soon it was time to go home again and out on the deck, I made the interesting discovery that the wind was gusting at 40 knots. Bearing in mind that the stalling speed of the Auster was a mere 28 knots, this made takeoff a novel proposition. I warned the deck crew to keep a tight hold of the wing struts as the aircraft was untied. I prepared for takeoff and was favoured with a bombardment of (to me) meaningless coloured lights from the bridge and frantic waving from the batmen. Ignoring these, I opened the throttle, the tail came up and the controls were fully responsive. I waved 'chocks and strut holders away'. We were airborne immediately. Almost instantaneously, I was high above the deck and level with the bridge, from where Commander Flying was waving in a friendly manner. The other aircraft followed and after making a circuit of the ship, we set course for base after a most enjoyable experience.

Towards the end of 1958, the Flight was joined by a detachment from 651 Light Aircraft Squadron Workshop REME, the first such to be established in the UK. The Auster AOP6 was a two/three seat air observation and general purpose light aircraft and was quite tricky to fly, having a tendency to drop a wing and spin, if the pilot stopped concentrating. However it performed magnificent service in expert hands for many years all over the world. It also featured a cockpit with a leathery smell "reminiscent of a 1.5 litre Wolseley Saloon" and a parking brake "clearly borrowed from a Ford Popular". It was followed by later marks, the AOP9 and AOP12. The Auster's 1950s saloon car ambience and that delightful aroma can be confirmed by inspection of XR244, the lovingly preserved AOP9 which is maintained in flying condition at Middle Wallop,

Auster AOP6 WE551, pictured on page 43 landing on an aircraft carrier, is seen in more usual surroundings, at RAF Aldergrove, about 1960.

R Burrows

Early army helicopters were fairly basic machines, certainly by 21st century standards. Saro Skeeter AOP12 XM562 is pictured at RAF Bishopscourt about 1960.

R Burrows

Army Aviation in Ulster

as part of the AAC Historic Flight.

The Austers were joined at Aldergrove by the Saunders Roe Skeeter in 1960, the first to arrive being XL766 in February. The Skeeter AOP12 was a small two seat helicopter designed to fulfil a similar role to the Auster. It was an important aircraft in that it pioneered the use of helicopters by the army beyond the very small numbers of Hoverfly R-6s and Sycamores used in the 1950s. The Skeeter was a highly manoeuvrable aircraft, but not necessarily always in the required direction! Some 64 were procured and it has been said that ". . . on the whole the beast was mastered as much by instinct as by intellect". The cockpit of the Skeeter was quite roomy under its inverted pudding bowl canopy. It needed to be, as the flight controls, knobs and switches were built on generous lines. It was powered by a variant of the Gypsy Major engine and had wooden, fabric-covered rotor blades. Colonel Michael Hickey summed up the Skeeter's qualities "Despite its almost total lack of military value, it taught us how to deploy rotary-wing in the field and was fun to fly, in temperate weather that is." Another Skeeter pilot wrote "Pilots had a love/hate relationship with the beast, a bit like the screw gunner and his mule."

In 1961, 13 Flight received a letter of congratulations from the Minister of Home Affairs for the excellent photographs which they had taken for incorporation in a special programme produced for the use of Her Majesty the Queen and Prince Philip, on the occasion of their visit to the Province in August.

13 Flight remained at Aldergrove until November 1962, when it was replaced by 2 Reconnaissance Flight, 2 Royal Tank Regiment, with similar aircraft. In September 1963, Aldergrove replaced Nutts Corner as the civil airport for Northern Ireland, though it continued to function as a military airfield also. In this period the parent regiment of the flight at Aldergrove was the resident armoured regiment at Omagh. Whenever possible pilots of that regiment were posted to the Flight.

The years from 1963 to 1969 were relatively quiet. The army aviation presence was maintained from November 1964 by the Queen's Dragoon Guards Air Squadron, which replaced its Skeeters and Austers with Sioux AH1 helicopters in August 1966, the last Skeeter to serve in the Province being XN340, which departed on 17th of the month. The final Auster was the AOP12, XP280.

This close-up shot of 'Clockwork Mouse' Sioux XT811 on the helipad at Omagh in November 1976 shows the basic facilities of these aircraft very clearly.

KA Boyd

21 July 1976 and 665 Squadron Sioux XT541 is seen in the air over Sydenham.

R Burrows

By the spring of 1969, six Sioux were being operated by the 17th/21st Lancers Air Squadron at Aldergrove (supported by eleven REME technicians), with a further four helicopters from the Prince of Wales Regiment based at RAF Ballykelly. The American-designed Westland Bell 47G Sioux light utility helicopter was produced under licence by Agusta in Italy and by Westland at Yeovil, and some 150 were eventually delivered to the Army, the first British-built example having flown in 1965. The 'Clockwork Mouse' gave valiant and valuable service during the first difficult years of the Troubles, despite not having been designed for the variety of tasks which it undertook. A great deal was learned empirically. It was a fairly basic machine, with a groundspeed not much in excess of 70 mph, comparable to the contemporary Austin 1800, which had the effect of making Northern Ireland seem like quite a large country. It could carry a very small payload and was not supplied with any sophisticated surveillance devices. Therefore, flying at 400–500 feet over a rioting mob with the Squadron Sergeant Major (or anyone else who was handy and willing) and a borrowed pair of binoculars, could concentrate the mind quite well. The bubble canopy gave a marvellous all-round view but did not provide a happy feeling of armoured security from anything fired in its general direction. Moreover, as there was no provision for a crewman there was no socket for the intercom plug of his helmet (sometimes there wasn't even a spare helmet!). Another interesting tasking was taking a police dog and its handler aloft. Sometimes the dog was the least of the pilot's problems; for a person of greater than bantam size, the curved door apertures required a degree of suppleness to negotiate. A Sioux pilot commented very succinctly on the job as he saw it:

> Can you get in and out of Forkhill RUC station compound with a section commander who is a hefty Scotsman and two full jerrycans of water, on a day when the air temperature is 22 degrees centigrade and can you do it again and again and again, all morning, with the CO, the mail, the laundry, a sick private and two men returning from R&R?

Another duty which devolved to the Sioux was the patrolling of lines of electricity pylons, which were a very tempting target. A three and a half million candle power Nitesun searchlight was attached and each pylon was illuminated and checked from a height of 1000 feet. There are plenty of pylons in Ulster; indeed a naval exchange helicopter pilot was once heard to remark "Northern Ireland seems to be held together by wires, but apart from that it's not too bad." The Nitesun could provide either a wide or a pinpoint beam and was adjusted

Army Aviation in Ulster

in focus and movement by means of a remote control box operated from within the helicopter. It also proved to be very effective when illuminating an area for casualty evacuation and, somewhat surprisingly, was a difficult target for a gunman to sight his rifle on. On at least one occasion the Nitesun was used for humanitarian duties. One night, a drunk, weaving his way into a well-known dangerous area, was illuminated and a radio message to the nearest ground patrol resulted in the solitary reveller being taken into protective custody. Another Sioux pilot, related of a morning spent with Sergeant Irvine of the Royal Ulster Constabulary. The sergeant, who was stationed at Castlederg, asked if he could have a flight in a helicopter. Once airborne they flew over idyllic and, for once, peaceful countryside. They spotted a sheep up to its neck in a bog. The pilot said "We can't let the poor beast suffer." The sergeant agreed and drew his Beretta from inside his flak jacket. That wasn't quite what the pilot had in mind, so he contacted the police station and described the markings on the ewe. On being told that it belonged to the 'Mountain men' neither the pilot nor the sergeant were too keen on paying a visit to the owners, so the pilot devised a cunning plan. He landed, dumped the door and strapped Sergeant Irvine to the starboard litter, face down. Then hovering over the doubtless bemused beast, the sergeant reached down and grabbed the ewe by the horns. Out it plopped from the mud and the last they saw of it was a somewhat grumpy animal making its way up the hillside.

Soon the increasing violence and civil disturbance resulted in the force being supplemented by the four Westland Scout AH1s of 8 Flight which were sent, in August 1969, to RAF Ballykelly in support of the troops and police in Londonderry and Omagh.

The Scout was a design of the Saunders-Roe company, later taken over by Westland. The prototype aircraft G-APNU first flew on 20 July 1958 and a production batch was ordered for the army in 1960. The Scout AH 1 began to enter service in 1963, the first of 150 examples for the AAC. It was much better suited to the casualty evacuation role than the Sioux, as a modified stretcher, cut to size, could be accommodated across the rear passenger

A lone Sioux overflies the Waterside, Londonderry, during the early 1970s. The double-deck Craigavon Bridge can be seen to the left while Ebrington Barracks is seen bottom right.

Museum of Army Flying

Opposite: A Westland Scout, with an Eagle patrol, over the lake at Castle Dillon House, Co Armagh, featured on the cover of the 1976 *AAC Journal*.

Cpl WA Bain RAOC

21 May 1975 and two Westland-built aircraft are seen at Sydenham. 663 Squadron Sioux XT543 'R' is shut down while Scout XW798 'H', callsign Army Air 376, prepares to depart over Belfast. The gasholder at Holywood's long since closed gasworks can be seen in the distance.

R Burrows

compartment. Casualties travelling by Sioux had been carried externally, on a litter attached to each of the landing skids, and wrapped in a nothing more than a blanket – a rather exposed and potentially frightening position – though external litters were often used on the Scout too. The Scout was also rather faster, with a cruising speed of 120–125 mph. A rugged and robust aircraft, it gave the AAC much more lifting capability.

As well as carrying out taxi work for senior officers, photographic surveys of RUC stations to enable Sappers to review their defences, overhead cover for bomb disposal squads, casualty evacuation and re-supply duties, the simple and sturdy Westland Scouts flew many 'Eagle Sorties'. Normally two helicopters took part – a Sioux carrying the patrol leader, with his four-man team in the Scout. The four soldiers sat back to back on the cabin floor, their legs dangling over the side with their feet resting on the skids, ready to disembark speedily on landing and with a panoramic view of the terrain below. The patrol's job was to mount stop-and-search operations on road traffic, to search farmhouses, carry out general surveillance on the border or simply to maintain an army

THE ARMY AIR CORPS JOURNAL

EAGLE FLIGHT — CASTLEDILLON
by Cpl W. A. Bain RAOC

1976

49

Army Aviation in Ulster

As Middle Wallop gate guardian, Westland Scout AH1 XT638 fulfils a very different role today to that of the view above dating from 1976, showing the aircraft leaving Bessbrook with a joint Royal Marines and 3 UDR 'Eagle' patrol.   *mirrorpix.com*

presence. Many flights were flown at low level to enable the rapid deployment of the patrol, particularly when the quarry was a moving vehicle. The pilots learned fast in an operational environment and a tour in Northern Ireland was regarded as very valuable exercise in finding out the capabilities of men and aircraft.

The first commanding officer of the Northern Ireland Regiment wrote:

> Hundreds of aircrewmen must by now have coaxed a bevy of excited, nervous soldiers into a doors-off Scout, deterred them from poking their rifles through the roof and created order out of a chaotic tangle of rucksacks, machine guns, radios and eagle harnesses.

Not all 'Eagle patrols' were completely successful. One day a Scout landed on a beach where a proud boat owner was applying undercoat, after having sanded the hull with great care. The pilot failed to appreciate the effect of his downwash on sand and any adjacent paintwork. The boat owner was even less appreciative of the fine coat of gritty material added to his handiwork! He ran over brandishing his paintbrush in a threatening manner, with the result that the Scout returned to base with its door coated in a tasteful shade of light blue. Others could take a joke. One night a smugglers cache was discovered by a patrol. A helicopter was called in to assist in its lawful seizure the following day, by which time the watchful smugglers had removed all the cases of spirits – apart from one miniature, left as a token of esteem.

Aircraft would be detached from the main bases to Bessbrook on standby duties, again a Sioux pilot comments:

> 0800 hours and I'm with 'D' Company of 1 Argyll and

Army aviation in Northern Ireland

Left: Westland Scout XV129 departs from the-then rudimentary HLS at Bessbrook sometime in the early 1970s.

Museum of Army Flying

Below: These three views of Scout XZ134 undergoing 'on-site' maintenance at a more organised-looking Bessbrook probably date from the latter years of the 1970s. Facilities were still basic, though.

Museum of Army Flying

51

Sutherland Highlanders. They want the mail to go round, take some Saracen spares as well, then pick up a corporal for an Eagle sortie. Sit at 2000 feet and watch a Scout skim the hedges below you, the infantry patrol sitting in the back with their feet on the skids. Eagling over, we head back to Bessbrook for a refuel and a swift Mars bar and Coke from the ever-open Bessbrook mess.

Until 1972 all aircraft recovery tasks were carried out by road using equipment and REME technicians from 702 MSRD at Aldergrove. On 24 June 1972 Sergeant DC Reid REME, Lance Corporal D Moon REME and Private C Stevenson Para were killed on their way to a downed helicopter when a landmine exploded beneath their vehicle as it was driving through the Glenshane Pass. Henceforth RAF support helicopters were used, with REME technicians preparing the aircraft for aerial recovery.

The deployment of AAC assets expanded considerably as the mayhem grew ever worse. In the summer of 1972, six Sioux of the 16th/5th Queen's Royal Lancers were based at Omagh. Long Kesh was the location for the five Scouts and five Sioux of 661 Squadron with five more Scouts and three Sioux from 664 Squadron at Aldergrove. Three of 664's Sioux were at Ballykelly, along with three more from 40 Commando Royal Marines. By 1973 some 15 Scouts, 23 Sioux and three Beavers were based at in the province. An experienced pilot on his third tour of duty in Northern Ireland remarked "The overall impression is of an organisation better equipped, trained and organised to do its task in support of the other arms and working at a much higher degree of pressure and effectiveness."

During this time an AAC presence could be found at five different locations – Aldergrove, on the eastern shores of Lough Neagh, Ballykelly, on the north coast, Omagh, to the west, Long Kesh, south of Belfast and, for a few years, Sydenham, which was close to the heart of Belfast.

Throughout the first half of the 1970s, until the arrival of the Gazelle in 1976, Ballykelly was the base for a detachment of between three and five Sioux. One of the early detachments was provided by 666 Squadron. *Air Pictorial* visited them in February 1970:

No.666 Squadron, operating from the far side of the airfield, shares a hangar and parks its helicopters alongside the lorries and Land Rovers of 24 Infantry Brigade. Personnel strength is 12 pilots and six aircrew observers, supported by ground handlers and REME technicians, who service and maintain the aircraft. Half the pilots are of officer rank and the other half sergeant pilots, they come from all corners of the British Army. For the present emergency in Northern Ireland, the

This is the view, looking east, of the airfield at Ballykelly, Co Londonderry, from a 655 Squadron Lynx. The shoreline of Lough Foyle can be seen encroaching to the left of the picture, with the Derry–Belfast railway crossing the western end of runway 09/27 and Binevenagh prominent in the distance.

5 Regt AAC

Squadron is divided into two flights. The area for which it is responsible covers the whole of Ulster except for Belfast. It has many roles.

The *Air Pictorial* reporter was fortunate enough to be given the opportunity to sample one of these for himself:

> One of the more important tasks during winter is the re-supply of signal establishments high in the hills. I was taken to one such station a thousand feet up on Mount Binevenagh. There, lashed by high winds and snow blowing across the Atlantic direct from Iceland, were three vehicles and a tent of the Royal Corps of Signals. Later in the afternoon we fought our way outside against a mini-blizzard and up to the helicopter landing point, marked by a dayglo plastic H. The snow and lashing hail suddenly stopped and in the brief break in the weather a Sioux darted in to land, flown by Sergeant Bob Timson.

At times the AAC was relieved by a flight of Royal Marine Commando aircraft, firstly Sioux and subsequently Gazelle. The last Sioux to deploy to Ballykelly were from 665 Squadron, which departed in April 1977, sandwiched between the first two Gazelle detachments, provided by 651 and 659 Squadrons. 655 Squadron became based at Ballykelly in 1982 and remained there as the resident AAC unit until 1991. A story is told of a goodwill mission to Rathlin Island when some surplus stores were swopped for local lobsters and crabs (but only the Sergeants' Mess knows the full details!)

Two Scouts of 8 Flight were sent to Omagh in August 1969, though detachments of the resident flight at Aldergrove had been sent to Omagh since earlier in the decade. One of the existing armoured car garages had been converted into a very adequate hangar. Thereafter, Scout detachments supported the Sioux of the resident armoured regiment in rotation – 17th/21st Lancers, 16th/5th Queen's Royal Lancers, 1 Royal Tank Regiment, 13th/18th Royal Hussars, 15th/19th King's Royal Hussars, 9th/12th Royal Lancers – until 3 Flight, with, firstly, Sioux and then Gazelles, took on the light helicopter role from 1976. The Operational Diary of Scout Flight 661 Squadron, contained in the squadron newsletter *The Canterbury Tales* gives a flavour of life at Omagh in the mid-seventies:

> Insert covering patrol while suspect culvert bomb inspected by ATO. ATO successfully defused one large smooth rock after crawling about for 2 hours in the pouring rain. ATO, patrol and helicopter all had sense of humour failure. Pilot delighted.
>
> Cow lift from beach at low tide on Lough Foyle. Cow

Now a static display at 7 Regiment's base at Netheravon, Wiltshire, Scout XV136 departs from Lisanelly Barracks, Omagh, in November 1976.

KA Boyd

Army Aviation in Ulster

These two views were taken at Lisanelly Barracks, Omagh, 17 years apart. Compare the December 1993 view of 665 Gazelle XZ307 (above) with the November 1976 one of Sioux XT811 and note the major improvements in aircrew and passenger comfort!

KA Boyd

saved. Cow delighted.

Pax to Belfast. Special Prosecutor and Judge flown to Musgrave Park Hospital to interview three girls who set themselves alight while arming incendiary bombs in toilet cubicle of pub. Oh dear what can the matter be?

With the formation of the Northern Ireland Regiment in 1979, 655 Squadron based Scouts and Gazelles at Omagh until moving to Ballykelly in 1982, so ending some 13 years of operational history.

Long Kesh was a wartime airfield, which later achieved notoriety under another name – HMP Maze. It functioned as a helicopter base for six years between 1973 and 1979. A mixture of Scouts and Sioux gave way from 1976 onwards to a regular rotation of six Scouts and six Gazelles. A good indication of life there may be gained from the 'Bosses Blurb' of *The Kesh News* 658 Edition, Winter 1976/7:

> We're all living in the rather desolate prefab atmosphere of the Maze prison, just outside the main secure compound. There's no point in pretending it's a masterpiece of town planning. The place has grown in a haphazard way to suit the changing circumstances of the last few years. We have a large hangar and very reasonable accommodation and recreation facilities, by Northern Ireland standards. Our aircraft operate in support of 3 Infantry Brigade. Their job is to destroy terrorism and restore stability in a large country area, stretching right across the southern part of the province. Aircraft and crews are detached to security forces' bases up to 35 miles away from The Kesh. Our aim is to produce the quickest possible reaction time for the ground troops we serve, in providing reconnaissance, deploying troops, moving supplies and evacuating casualties. In the most active areas we get a helicopter in the air within three minutes of a request for our help – by day or night. None of this would be possible without the hard work and technical skill of our LAD. Our nut stranglers work a 24 hour shift on alternate days. As always, they're proving expert at producing the goods to a high standard, in all sorts of situations.

Sydenham (now Belfast City Airport) was home to a succession of Royal Marine Commando and AAC Sioux detachments from February 1973 until August 1976; thereafter the final two tours were undertaken by the Gazelles of 3 Commando Brigade Air Squadron, until the withdrawal from this base in October 1977. From 1969 Sydenham had also been the location of the prison ship HMS *Maidstone*, moored at Airport Wharf. From time to time a safe haven was also provided for Belfast Corporation buses and bin lorries, which otherwise were a soft target for rioters.

The major permanent location for the AAC in Ulster has, undoubtedly, been Aldergrove, with the succession of Austers, Skeeters, Sioux, Scouts, Beavers, Gazelles, Lynx and Islanders from 1957 to the present day. As the earlier shorter-range helicopters were replaced by more modern and capable aircraft, it made sense to concentrate the resources at one location, which gave the advantage of centralised operational control, spares and servicing. Naturally, Aldergrove was the most suitable spot, as will be related later in this account. The change was not

An unidentified Sioux arrives at Aldergrove with the 23 MU hangars in the background.

Museum of Army Flying

6 Flight DHC Beaver XP819 is shown departing from Sydenham, now Belfast City Airport, on 13 August 1975.

R Burrows

necessarily the most popular of moves with those at the sharp end, as immediate contact with the troops in the field was lost, together with a certain amount of autonomy of action.

The effectiveness and utility of the helicopters was much appreciated by the ground troops. These rotary-wing types were soon to be joined by a great Army Air Corps workhorse, the DHC-2 Beaver, a tough high-wing monoplane much loved by bush pilots worldwide. It first flew in August 1947 and 1631 were sold, including 46 to the Army, entering service in 1964. The Beavers came on detachment, firstly with a single aircraft only, early in 1972. The initial detachment of three aircraft was provided by 655 Squadron in October 1973. Further detachments were made by 3 Flight and 669 Squadron until the establishment of the Beaver Flight of five aircraft at Aldergrove in March 1976. They were a very reliable, robust aircraft and a joy to fly, but it is undeniable that they were also not very fast and rather noisy. They were powered by a 450 hp Pratt and Whitney engine and had an excellent short takeoff capability. WO2 Chris Sherlock believes that he holds the world record for the slowest flight between Middle Wallop and Aldergrove – five and a half hours, with no autopilot (this did not feature on the Beavers' equipment list), using a navigational 'computer' that had to be "beaten into submission" before it worked. In practised hands, however, the Decca Navigator was a useful and reliable aid, especially in poor visibility and for blind landings. There are few Beaver pilots who do not have fond memories of this chunky, practical, powerful 'flying Land Rover' and who would not like to fly it just one more time. A party piece of the experienced Beaver pilot at Aldergrove was to complete a landing on the piano keys at the threshold of the runway.

Flying the Beaver in the Province was not without hazard, as Major NJ 'Sam' Law discovered one day, when, in the course of being shot at from the ground, a round severed the intercom lead at the back of his co-pilot's helmet and passed out through the windscreen. The bullet-holed propeller has been preserved, as have photographs of the gunmen at work. As OC of the Beaver Flight, Major Law was well-qualified on the aircraft, with over 5000 hours on type, which included more than 300 crossings of the Irish Sea.

Initially, photographic reconnaissance of marches, demonstrations and rallies was carried out by the helicopter crews, using hand held cameras and later a specially-designed, vibration-damped mounting. Whilst the results were often very good, the more specialised fixed camera in the Beaver was a better long term solution for a range of vital tasks. The cameras were mounted on standard NATO bomb racks fitted beneath the Beavers' wings. All went well until one day one of these operated as intended and deposited an expensive camera onto the runway at Aldergrove.

The deployment of helicopters for four month tours of duty came under the title of 'Operation Banner'. For a period of ten years between 1969 and 1979 (when the Northern Ireland Regiment was formed) the following AAC squadrons undertook tours of duty, some of them many times – 651, 652, 653, 654, 655, 657, 658, 659, 660, 661, 662, 663, 664, 665, 666 and 669. Many of the squadrons produced newsletters, which varied greatly in style, format, content, quality and degree of political correctness. They were very useful as morale-building tools in an environment where it was not possible to live any sort of a normal social life. They convey the flavour and spirit of the AAC in Ulster over the course of a decade or more by means of articles, poems, puns, jokes, cartoons and photographs. The titles were sometimes simply derived from the squadron's location – *The Ballykelly Bugle, The Kesh News*; others were more prosaic – *Op Banner Times*, or *xxx Squadron Newsletter*. 665 had *The Snipe* but the prize for inventiveness must go to 655 Squadron for *Nitesun, Rotorvator* and the *Psyclik Magazine*.

Flying hours were often well in excess of the more usual peacetime limit of fifty hours per month. An extension to permit 220 hours within a three month period was authorised, later being increased to 230 hours. During the early 1970s, the six Sioux based at Omagh would regularly clock up 270 hours a month between them, though as a report at a REME engineering conference noted, aircraft availability was high despite the increased flying rate and the considerable strain on the maintainers. It was remarked that:

There are many ways to leave the Province following an 'Op Banner' tour, as the-then 'Floppy QHI', SSgt 'Beaker' Williams well knows!
5 Regt AAC

'The imaginary line.' Sgts Cammack and Pye and Cpl Baines with Lynx XZ641 overfly an observation post close to the Armagh/Louth border on 26 August 2001.
KA Boyd

Surely it proves firstly, what one has always suspected, that things go better when they are used and that although scheduled servicings must increase in direct proportion to the flying rate, the unscheduled does not.

It was added, however, that in order to ensure flight safety remaining paramount, "It is not only pilot fatigue we have to watch but also technician fatigue."

Some idea of the complexity of the job beyond the flying task (which was demanding enough in itself) may be gained from considering communications. Contact had to be maintained with civil Air Traffic Control on a range of frequencies, with other military aircraft on a different radio and additionally, tactical matters required discussion with the ground troops on yet a third system. While keeping on top of this, a strict eye had to be kept on the helicopter's exact location, particularly on duties close to the border. The imaginary line between Northern Ireland and the Irish Republic follows many apparently arbitrary and tortuous twists and turns for 303 miles as the crow would certainly not fly. A moment's lack of concentration could result in a potentially diplomatically embarrassing incursion. The border placed a major constraint on aerial activities; it was effectively an impenetrable barrier for the security forces but not so for those seeking to make incursions and then return to safety.

A more detailed look at one 'Op Banner' tour made by a detachment of 657 Aviation Squadron, between February and June 1972, may serve to give a flavour of an experience common to hundreds of AAC personnel over the years. The squadron was based at Soltau in what was then still West Germany, when in October 1971 it was detailed to provide six of its ten aircraft for duty in Ulster, for the planned Eastern Armoured Reconnaissance Regiment. Two weeks ground training was given in

14 February 1971 and 657 Aviation Squadron Sioux 'F' is loaded into the hold of a Shorts 'Belfast' freighter at Hannover en route to Northern Ireland.

Brigadier E Tait

January, covering a wide range of skills including basic internal security tactics, map reading, bombs and explosives, anti-ambush drills, fitness, first aid, road blocks and searches, driving and signals, PR and photography. In addition some considerable time was devoted to weapons training and range work. Flying training covered detailed map reading exercises, car chases, area searches, casevac, underslung loads and night flying. In addition two lectures were given by pilots with recent experience in the Province. The six Sioux were flown from Hannover to Aldergrove in two RAF Belfast freighters on 14 and 15 February. Within an hour and a half they had been re-

Army Aviation in Ulster

Acting Major Edward Tait at the controls of Sioux XT566 'G' over Newry.

Brigadier E Tait

A very rare colour view of Sioux 'F', the aircraft featured on page 59, taken at Gosford Castle, Markethill, Co Armagh, in 1972.

Brigadier E. Tait

Opposite : 'Mutual Support 1'. With the slopes of Feede Mountain and the border behind 7 Squadron's Chinook, 665 Squadron Lynx XZ663 and ZA704 'J' overfly the Belfast–Dublin railway just north of Moore's Bridge, near Drumintee, en route to Forkhill.

Museum of Army Flying

assembled and were ready to fly to the Detachment's home, for the next four months, at Long Kesh. (REME commented that they eventually took off two hours later as the pilots were at lunch!).

On first sight Long Kesh was a dismal spot:

> . . . sprawled over and around a disused airfield. Everything seemed to be either half built or half demolished and the whole complex wallowed in a sea of mud. Unkempt huts and caravans scattered apparently at random; half a draughty hangar peppered with holes.

Unfavourable comparisons were made with the comforts enjoyed by the residents of the adjoining internment camp ". . . heated rooms, a television set in every room, hobbies rooms, recreation and sports areas, three good meals a day and no rent to pay."

By 17 February three aircraft had flown ten hours of operational sorties with ". . . no tools, no oil, no grease, no paperwork, a hangar full of rubbish and an LAD office full of water." The 'can do' spirit was alive and well but it shows that in the early days AAC units, and especially REME, had to 'make-do and mend' as best they could.

The squadron's area of operations included a long and active section of the border – Newry, Forkhill, Crossmaglen and Newtownhamilton. The main Belfast to Dublin road and railway line ran through the area, together with many other cross border routes, both approved and unapproved. The eastern half of the patch included the Mountains of Mourne and a substantial stretch of coastline.

Almost all operational sorties were flown in support of troops on the ground. The OC produced a list of these for his Post Tour Report:

> Recces of border, border incidents, border crossing blocks, suspect cars, areas to select observation posts, areas prior to cordons and searches, buildings prior to 'lifts' of wanted men, suspected booby traps, routes for claymore devices, specific wanted vehicles, hijacked cars and lorries (often burning), sniper locations, meetings, marches, funerals, public gatherings, recce parties for newly arrived units, Eagle flights with Wessex. Casevac. Photography of bomb damage, for operational planning, border crossing points and public gatherings. Liaison – flying commanders to their scattered sub unit locations, to the scene of incidents and with high priority documents.

This represented the daytime commitment only. During the hours of darkness a Nitesun aircraft had to be available for call out at minimal notice to illuminate landing sites for Scout or Wessex, to light up civil disturbances, night searches for snipers and wanted vehicles, night 'lifts' and, once, to search for a ship reported by the RN minesweeper patrol vessel to be approaching the coast without lights.

It is small wonder therefore that the seven pilots accumulated approaching 300 flying hours each during the tour, the equivalent of a normal yearly total in one third of the time. This had its penalties – missed meals, continual early starts and late finishes, weekends which didn't exist. It could not have been achieved without the phenomenal effort of the REME technicians, whom the OC praised for their outstanding support.

The OC also commented on the preparation required for a Banner tour:

> On arrival we were very much in the dark on techniques used in the theatre. This was in part due to the lack of any aviation SOPs (Standard Operating Procedures). After much ferreting for information and a few weeks' experience, the Squadron produced its own. There were very few techniques which could not be readily assimilated. There was, however, a mass of detail, which together with local knowledge could go a long way to making flying operations in the theatre both safer and more effective.

Some individual experiences included the day the duty pilot had to convey five pilots, five observers and 4000 rounds of ammunition to the range at Magilligan Point, on the north coast, and back, and still carry out the normal daily tasks. This knotty problem was solved with the help of a slide rule and a Scout from 664 Squadron. On another occasion a helicopter was approaching Forkhill to land when the message came over the radio "Hello X61A this is J2 you have just been shot at five times....wait....six times, over." Then there were the car hunts, which always seemed to be for a blue Cortina, when every fourth car on the ground appeared to be a similar make and colour; the saloon car packed with 400 lbs of explosive that demolished half a petrol filling station and, tragically, the murdered UDR corporal whose body was dumped back in the North with 600 lbs of gelignite attached. There were happier moments – 4000 cakes and sponges baked by the ladies of Portadown and then there were school children who held a jumble sale and used the money raised to buy books and cigarettes for the squadron.

Much effort was expended at Long Kesh to try and make it a little more habitable – a badminton-cum-volleyball court was marked out and a table tennis table was acquired, a flower garden was created outside the squadron building, works services were chivvied into action and a squadron magazine, *The Siouxerat*, was produced, with specially drawn cartoons by Hargreaves.

At the end of the tour the detachment was commended by the GOC Northern Ireland for its hard work and the OC was praised for ". . . the camp and conditions under which they lived having been improved beyond all recognition."

660 Squadron were based at Long Kesh in 1973 with a mixed force of Sioux and Scouts and commented on activities noticed while flying over south Armagh:

> The livelihood of many of the people is dependant on the border. Fortunes are made by raising pigs on one side of the border and selling them on the other or by stripping old cars and selling the components in Dublin. One of our greatest successes was apprehending a lorry load of carrots which was trying to creep into the North along an unapproved road. The beauty of the area is marred by the fact that every farm and house seems to have a flourishing scrapyard in the back garden.

The squadron flew response teams into firefights when attacks were made on the police stations in Crossmaglen and Forkhill. Small arms, mortar rounds and RPG 7 rockets were directed at the stations but the only real casualty was a tracker dog who had his kennel demolished and suffered traumatic shock. In another incident the Dublin to Belfast train was hijacked and a bomb placed on board. It was detonated by a marksman with a well-aimed shot, which was one way of making a controlled explosion! An involuntary incursion was made across the border which was reported in the *Irish People* of Saturday 16 June 1973:

> A British Army helicopter landed at the farm of Mr James Faughey yesterday. He was questioned by four armed paratroopers about a County Louth registered car which was in the yard. When he told them that it was registered in the Republic because he lived in the Republic they cleared off. Later Mr Faughey said, 'I saw

at least ten other uniformed men in the helicopter. They must have known they were in the Republic because the pilot had a map.

It is possible he may well have been exaggerating the Scout's payload but he certainly showed a touching faith in the map reading skills of the squadron's pilots.

Creature comforts at Long Kesh were enhanced by the establishment of a menagerie – two goats, a brace of ducks, a pair of racing pigeons and eight trout in the static water tank. The fish were fed with worms:

> . . . caught by our patent electrical worming machine designed by the REME. This device when stuck in the ground and switched on, ensured that every local worm within a five foot radius suddenly dropped everything and shot to the surface.

Keeping to technical matters, the 100 or more REME technicians based in the province by the mid-70s had to cope with a range of special-to-theatre role equipment, which they were trained to service 'on the job'. Considerable ingenuity was required, for example, infrared searchlights were improvised from Chieftain spotlights and Land Rover headlights. Locally produced solutions to operational problems had to be designed, developed and engineered and help was given by RAF Maintenance Unit personnel at Sydenham and Aldergrove. The results were often so good that they gained general acceptance beyond the confines of the province.

Aerial reconnaissance by helicopter became more sophisticated with the introduction of shoulder-mounted television cameras, operated by the observer. To begin, the images were in black and white only. Then a remotely controlled, stabilised camera – attachable to the underside of the machine – was developed and colour transmission became possible. Passive Night Goggles (PNG) were introduced in 1976, which enabled many tasks to be completed more quickly, more safely and more effectively.

Towards the end of the 1970s, the Sioux was no longer part of the scene. Sergeant Howard Gater-Smith RTR composed a valedictory poem while serving with the Scots Dragoon Guards at Long Kesh:

> To those of you who are Ireland bound,
> A point or two that we have found,
> Might help prevent many a tear,
> Sometime in this coming year.
>
> Give some thought to the All up Weight,
> Don't forget the armour plate,
> Remember Nitesun and Dectrac,
> Plus those bulky jackets flak.
>
> Fly above a thousand feet,
> Fear not, no jets will you meet,
> Beware the border and scrapyard spots,
> From both many a Paddy has taken pots!
>
> The weather also has its quirks,
> Don't get caught out like other berks,
> Beware low cloud and swirling fog,
> And surely many hours you'll log.
>
> With greetings to all from Scots DG,
> This information is all quite free,
> Till February then and much glee,
> The Sioux of 657 we'll be pleased to see!

Sadly, the last years of the Sioux saw two crashes, in the first of which, in 1975, Major JD Hicks was killed. The second was in 1977, when the helicopter hit some overhead wires and dropped into the River Bann minus its rotor assembly. It was retrieved and airlifted out by the strenuous efforts of a team of Royal Engineer divers.

The final deployment of Sioux were those belonging to 652 Squadron – XT102, XT558 and XT815 – which were based at Aldergrove from August to December 1977.

The next major change was the formation of the Northern Ireland Regiment AAC on 1 November 1979, under the command of Lieutenant Colonel DJ Ralls DFC. This logical and sensible development provided a formal command structure and administrative infrastructure to support the flying task. Instead of 16 AAC squadrons rotating on tours of duty through the province (some as many as seven times in ten years), proper provision was made to enable greater efficiency in the use of the resources available. BAOR AAC Regimental HQ involvement also ceased, with the withdrawal of 4 Regiment from Aldergrove in December and the last detachment of Scouts on roulement from Germany. The rotation of squadrons did not cease but the pressure was eased by the permanent presence of 655 Squadron. The first aircraft to join the new regiment were the four Scouts of 655 Squadron's Scout Flight, which arrived from Topcliffe at the end of October. Another significant event

Army Aviation in Ulster

The final three Sioux in Northern Ireland transit along the north shore of Belfast Lough and overfly Black Head lighthouse, Islandmagee, on their departure from the Province in December 1977. Can any AAC personnel furnish details of the aircrew?

Museum of Army Flying

655 Squadron's Scouts are seen arriving at Aldergrove to join their Gazelle colleagues and 654 Squadron's Lynx AH1s to form the Northern Ireland Regiment AAC in October 1979.

5 Regt AAC

in the same year was the arrival of the rest of the squadron's Scouts along with six Gazelles, with these helicopters being based at Lisanelly Barracks, Omagh.

The Westland Lynx AH 1 was introduced in October 1979 with the deployment of aircraft from 654 Squadron to Aldergrove on a four month tour of duty. They operated mostly from Armagh and St Angelo (Enniskillen). The main advantages of the Lynx were the increased safety offered by its twin-engine configuration, its greater speed – up to 150 kts – and its faster reaction time, with five minutes from call out to takeoff. The good power margin ensured excellent performance at maximum all-up weight and the ability to operate in higher wind conditions. Payload and endurance were also an improvement on the Scout. It was equipped with more modern avionics and, in particular, the Decca Tactical Air Navigation System (TANS). This equipment gave the Lynx a good day/night, all-weather, low-visibility capability. It also reduced the crew workload, allowing more time to be given to tactical matters and actually flying the aircraft. During that first deployment from October to February, when Northern Ireland's weather is arguably at its worst, the Lynx of 654 Squadron achieved 98% of their allocated hours and only once failed to provide 24-hour cover at one of its principal bases. Less welcome characteristics were the rather slippery cabin floor, design faults with the cabin doors, the rather too-delicate tail skid and the tendency of the aircraft to leave an oily mark as evidence of its presence on a landing pad.

Comparative figures produced by REME at Headquarters Northern Ireland (HQNI) illustrate the high usage and efficiency of the other types of aircraft deployed in the Province at that time:

Scout	NI flying rate	59.3	Availability	93.6%
	Elsewhere	21.1		73.9%
Gazelle	NI flying rate	64.1	Availability	83.6%
	Elsewhere	25.3		74.0%
Beaver	NI flying rate	48.0	Availability	89.0%
	Elsewhere	25.1		83.2%

A well-known but mythical figure around Alexander Barracks at Aldergrove during this period was a certain Airtrooper Hooper. His somewhat lax attitude to the proper procedures regarding booking out and in was a source of great annoyance to the RSM of the Scots Guards and of innocent pleasure to the AAC. The perpetrators met their downfall one evening, when a little the worse for wear, they decided to scale the exterior of the RSM's pride and joy – a brand new inflatable gym. They painted on the top, especially for passing helicopters, "Airtrooper Hooper was here". Sadly they had not realised that the roof was translucent and that their handiwork was visible from the inside. Climbing the gym wall again in daylight, stone cold sober, with supplies of paint remover and brushes was their reward.

In 1979 a Royal Military Policewoman, based at Armagh, had a never-to-be-forgotten experience of Army aviation, her account of the incident beginning:

> Early one morning, having lent my female presence to a dawn house search, I was to be transported home by helicopter. On approaching the machine I faced the problem of installing myself in the front seat encumbered by short stature and a tight uniform skirt. The back seat was occupied by two RUC men either side of a prisoner and the rotors were turning. I proceeded to enter the helicopter by first attempting to kneel on the floor in front of the seat. Due to a momentary, involuntary and unexpected shift in my centre of gravity I started to overbalance. With lightning instinct I grabbed for a handhold; unfortunately I grabbed the collective pitch lever and the helicopter took off. The pilot was surprised and so was one of the RUC men and so was I. The pilot started to pilot and the RUC man and I fell out.
>
> With the skill of his breed the pilot landed the helicopter. I recommenced the mounting procedure; the pilot appeared to be congratulating me but due to the engine noise I could not catch the exact form of his compliments. I then noticed an RUC constable knocking on the helicopter door by the pilot's head. He was alternately knocking and pointing downwards in what appeared to be a mixture of pain, annoyance and shock. This seemed to me a silly attitude; he had not fallen from a great height – well not a very great height – and should just get back in the aircraft and say nothing, like the gentleman I took him to be.
>
> I was surprised when the helicopter rose into the air once more but it became clear that the manoeuvre was necessary to free the policeman's foot. He was not only so careless as to place his foot under the skid of the landing helicopter but is still being unreasonable and unforgiving about the whole incident.
>
> The author would be pleased to hear from the pilot or

The Royal Military Policewoman's view? 655 Squadron Lynx XZ673 departs from Bessbrook on 15 September 1997.

KA Boyd

RUC man with their version of events.

The courage of the Army Air Corps is aptly illustrated by an incident on 26 November 1981. Sergeant Ian Shoebridge, of 654 Squadron, was coming to the end of a five-month tour. That dark and stormy evening his Lynx was based at St Angelo, Enniskillen, on a 24-hour duty, when a report came through of a large explosion. A bomb had been detonated at the vehicle checkpoint at Mullinbridge, close to the border, injuring four soldiers and four civilians. Local communications were also down due to the destruction of telephone wires and radio masts. Shoebridge took off, despite the deteriorating weather, with a six-man Airborne Reaction Force, a doctor and assistant. On arrival at the scene, the team started to look for the casualties, while Shoebridge illuminated the area with his 'Nitesun'. The casualties were then airlifted to St Angelo, where the helicopter refuelled. It was decided that they had to be taken to hospital in Belfast. The cloud base had lowered and the Lynx was given radar assistance from RAF Aldergrove. Breaking cloud at 500 feet, Shoebridge followed the road to Musgrave Park Hospital, where the most seriously injured man received immediate surgery. Ian Shoebridge was awarded the Air Force Medal for his actions, the citation stating that "He had proved himself an outstanding aviator whose calm and cool handling of the situation had made possible a very difficult casualty evacuation in deteriorating weather conditions".

During the first three years of its existence the Northern Ireland Regiment consisted of the Beaver Flight, the 655 Squadron Scout Flight and the roulement squadron of Lynx and Gazelles – all based at Aldergrove – together with the Scouts and Gazelles of 655 Squadron at Omagh. Three Gazelles of the Royal Marines at Ballykelly also came under the control of the Regiment. The aircraft were maintained and supported by 70 Aircraft Workshop Detachment REME and 3 Mobile Stores Detachment

'Scout – N.I. Flying rate 59.3%. Availability 93.6%' (though sometimes with assistance! – on this occasion from 72 Squadron RAF Wessex XT669 'T'.)

Museum of Army Flying

RAOC, both located at Aldergrove.

The next type to depart from operational duties was the Westland Scout, in October 1982. Just before 655 Squadron replaced its Scouts with the Lynx AH1, it became based at Ballykelly and the Aldergrove Scout flight converted to Gazelles. While 655 Squadron was working up to operational status with the Lynx, cover was provided by a Lynx detachment from 669 Squadron.

On 1 October 1982, a special lunch was held in Hangar 151 at Aldergrove to celebrate the AAC Silver Jubilee. Some 200 attended and at the end of the meal the last Scout task in Northern Ireland was carried out by Major MA Jones, in XT623, flying guests back to HQNI at Lisburn.

Perhaps the greatest contribution made by the Scout was the establishment of what became the best known and most-frequented social club in the history of Aldergrove. It was set up by the original Scout Flight in the forward section of the abandoned fuselage of Vickers Varsity WJ898/N, next door to a portacabin which housed the Beaver Flight office. When the fuselage was dismantled the portacabin became the Beaver Bar. A memento of the past is retained, as a propeller from the Varsity is displayed to this day outside the 1 Flight offices. During its heyday in the 1980s the Beaver Bar was the hub of activity and was open to all ranks and all services – with the result that joint operations and co-operation improved considerably; it could be argued that it was the first Joint Helicopter Force (Northern Ireland) HQ! Its Christmas Draw became legendary for the fantastic prizes offered from all around the province and The Beaver Bar's passing was mourned by many.

Many and varied tasks fell to the aircraft of the regiment – schoolboys lost when hill walking on the Antrim Plateau were airlifted to safety; a diabetic farmer who had gone missing was found at night with the aid of

This manufacturer's photograph of a Westland Scout AH1 is included to show the type in 'as delivered' condition.

Westland Helicopters Ltd

This 1982 shot of Vickers Varsity WJ898 'N' on the Aldergrove fire dump was taken before it assumed its role as the famous 'Beaver Bar'.

R Burrows

the Nitesun carried by a Lynx operating from St Angelo, Enniskillen; seven people were rescued from a cabin cruiser when it ran into rocks on Lough Erne; a diver suffering from the 'bends' was taken from Lough Swilly, in the Irish Republic, to Craigavon Hospital and a cow was plucked from a bog at the bottom of a ravine. Great flying skill was required in all these incidents but perhaps none more so than in the case of the unconscious schoolgirl, taking part in a Duke of Edinburgh's Silver Award Scheme expedition, who was rescued from a mountain top near Ballycastle. As the girl was too ill to be moved any distance on foot and the mountain covered in cloud, the pilot had to hover-taxi his aircraft up the side of the mountain, through dense fog, to the rendezvous. The aircrewman then moved forward on foot to the injured girl, guided by whistle blasts from her companions. Once she was safely on board, the pilot took off in cloud and made an instrument recovery into Aldergrove. The former MP, Bernadette McAliskey, and her husband were attacked and injured by gunmen at their isolated home near Coalisland. Only a timely airlift by Lynx, and a rapid transfer to hospital, saved her life. Considerable assistance was given to the farming community in south Armagh on many occasions during cold and wintry weather, when drifting snow cut off farms and separated farmers from their cattle.

Weather was also a factor on another occasion. Regimental Commanding Officers are always very experienced pilots but their heavy workload tends to mean that they are more conversant with the complexities of running the regiment rather than cockpit management skills. One Christmas, the CO embarked on his usual aerial visit to his men on duty around the province. The Lynx Squadron Commander elected to fly him; the aircrewman felt that this was not necessarily a sound move, as the Major's most recent flying had been chiefly of his desk! All went well to begin with until on the way to Bessbrook, it began to rain and then snow rather heavily. The CO made the helpful suggestion that it would probably be a good idea to turn on the windscreen wipers. After some quiet contemplation, firstly one and then two pairs of hands made an ever more frantic scrabble around the instrument panel in a vain attempt to locate the relevant switch. The aircrewman observed all

Shades of 13 Flight and HMCS *Bonaventure* – a 655 Squadron Lynx is pictured practicing deck landings on RFA *Fort George* during Exercise 'Scottish Wave' in January 2001.

5 Regt AAC

RFA *Fort George* is through the cockpit window of a Lynx during Exercise 'Scottish Wave'.

5 Regt AAC

but, wisely, kept silent, not wishing to parade his superior knowledge. Having exhausted the possibilities and abandoning the option of pressing or flipping something to see what happened, the CO then said to the major "Well, if you switch on the TANS, we would at least know where we are." If turning on the wipers had proved too technical an operation, then the chances of locating, initiating and programming the navigational system were slim indeed. The major had a brainwave, and with the speed of light he replied "Sorry Sir, it's Christmas Day and the Americans will have turned off all their satellites." Full marks indeed for quick thinking but none for truth or accuracy. The aircrewman dined out on the story for months afterwards.

The Beaver Flight made the headlines in 1986, when a superb formation photograph featured as the cover of the *AAC Journal*. A year later more headlines were achieved, when a Beaver created quite a stir by flying 40 miles into the Irish Republic. A cartoon in an Irish newspaper put the matter in perspective. A bemused pilot is being questioned by an officer of the Garda Siochana – "And what would a chap like you be doing down here? Member of the Irish soccer team are we, Sir?" This was a reference to the then manager of the Irish football team, Jack

Four DHC Beavers are recorded on the cover of the 1986 Journal.

Sgt D Hayward RAOC

Charlton, who was very creative in finding Irish antecedents for his players.

Also in 1986, 665 Squadron was reformed at Aldergrove and became part of the Northern Ireland Regiment, equipped initially with a mix of Gazelles and Lynx. With specific Lynx airframes being set aside for the task in the Province, the time-consuming need to strip out and replace the specialised anti-tank equipment needed for the Lynx's role in Germany was avoided. With two full squadrons now permanently based in Northern Ireland the need for the short term roulement of units also came to an end.

Moreover the REME assets were also reorganised, with the creation of the Northern Ireland Regiment Workshop at Aldergrove. This subsumed the work of 70 Aircraft Workshop Detachment, the Beaver Flight and 665 Squadron's LAD. The first Officer Commanding was Major Bernie Guignard. Roulement troops were now trickle posted, rather than arriving as formal squadrons, which eased the burden. 655 Squadron's LAD remained at Ballykelly. Some idea of REME's skill and dedication may be gained from a very tricky operation at night the following year. In foul weather, and in ". . . a dangerous place close to the border", the main rotor gearbox of a stricken Lynx was replaced by a REME team in the field where it had come to rest. High rates of flying, as well as changes of role and payload, placed quite a strain on the Workshop. For their efforts, Major Guignard and his Artificer Sergeant Major (ASM), Warrant Officer Class 1 Phil Hall, were awarded MBEs.

Some idea of the level to which AAC operations had grown by the end of the 1980s may be gained from the scale of operations at Northern Ireland's, and indeed Europe's, busiest heliport – Bessbrook Mill, near Newry – the focal point of the security forces' operations in south Armagh and along the border with the Irish Republic.

15 September 1997 was a busy day at Bessbrook. A passenger from 1 Bn Welsh Guards watches the camera as Lynx XZ673 returns with XZ615 in the background.

KA Boyd

Army Aviation in Ulster

In this view 655 Squadron Lynx XZ218 is pictured leaving the 'well' helipad at Bessbrook on 19 June 1996.

KA Boyd

RAF and AAC helicopters amassed over 600 flights a week in and out of Bessbrook – on average one every eight minutes during daylight hours – and as many as 15,000 passengers a month. Since 1972 this village has probably seen more army fliers than any other, save Middle Wallop.

In 1991 655 Squadron moved from Ballykelly, joining 665 Squadron at Aldergrove.

On 1 October 1993, the Northern Ireland Regiment AAC was retitled 5 Regiment AAC. The new regiment's facilities at Aldergrove were involved in a plan conceived in the mid-1990s to renew the army's connection with lighter-than-air aviation – in the bulbous shape of ZH762, a Westinghouse Skyship 500. This airship was flown by AAC pilots in the course of an extensive trials programme. It had the advantages of being able to lift a considerable quantity of mission-related equipment and of being able to remain in the air for protracted periods of time. Against these benefits had to be set the undeniable facts that it was slow, not being capable of more than 30–40 kts and that it was not well-suited to windy or icy weather conditions. Useful experience was gained but the province has not been graced in subsequent years by an airship unit. As an historical footnote it may be noted that during the First World War the Royal Naval Air Service operated coastal patrol airships from Bentra, near Whitehead in County Antrim.

In 1995 5 Regiment was granted permission by the Army Air Corps Regimental Committee to adopt the motto of the Glider Pilot Regiment – 'Nothing is Impossible'. On 30 June 1995 the Regiment exercised the privilege of Trooping the Guidon through the ranks, as part of a Beating the Retreat parade at Aldergrove. The GOC Northern Ireland, Lieutenant General Sir Roger Wheeler KCB, CBE took the salute, with the Director of

Westinghouse Skyship 500 ZH762 is seen at 5 Regiment's Aldergrove base during its visit in 1995. Seven years later it was exported to the USA.

5 Regt AAC

Gazelle XZ345 'M' of 2 Regiment's 671 Squadron and 1 Flight Islander ZG993 are pictured at the dispersal adjacent to Hangar 3 at Middle Wallop on 14 August 2002.

KA Boyd

Army Aviation in Ulster

Army Aviation, Major General SW StJ Lyttle and the Commanding Officer of 5 Regiment, Lieutenant Colonel Richard Folkes in attendance. Musical accompaniment was provided by the Band of the Army Air Corps. As the Guidon halted by the parade commander, the band played Sunset, the flags were lowered and a flypast of two Lynx, two Gazelles and an Islander passed overhead. In the words of Rudyard Kipling "A band revives memories, it quickens associations, it opens and unites the hearts of men more surely than any other appeal can."

Suitably attired for the conditions, soldiers from 1 Bn Devon and Dorset Regiment board Lynx XZ615 on 30 December 2000. Compare this view with that on page 71, taken three years earlier, when the same aircraft was on the adjacent spot.

KA Boyd

Part 3: 5 Regiment Army Air Corps

The Regiment's main role is to support the security forces in Northern Ireland – the British Army and the Police Service of Northern Ireland (PSNI). For command purposes, the army in Ulster is divided into three main areas coterminous with police regions – 8 Infantry Brigade covers the north and west, which includes Londonderry and Enniskillen, 3 Brigade is responsible for the south and east – Armagh and Newry – and 39 Brigade's patch extends around Greater Belfast and to the north as far as Larne. 5 Regiment comprises some 43 aircraft and more than 370 men and women. It is large in terms of the monetary value of its hardware and medium-sized regarding personnel strength. The Regiment scores very highly in respect of the calibre of its soldiers and also in terms of their workrate and efficiency; the taxpayer is gaining full value from the efforts of all ranks. There is a definite buzz about the regiment – it has a job to do and is well-resourced to fulfil the task. The high morale that comes from having a sense of purpose is evident. The 'can do' spirit is palpable, getting the job done, and done well, is the aim. All ranks work long hours and take on a high level of responsibility.

With fewer troops on the ground, there is a greater focus on what can be achieved in the air. Observation and monitoring tasks are vitally important in giving stability to what everyone hopes will become a permanent transition to peace and normality. The component sub-units have their own individual character. 655 Squadron is a punchy outfit, taking the lead 'down south' (south Armagh), creating a presence with the noisy, powerful, responsive

'South Armagh scenery 1.' This view of 655 Squadron Lynx XZ641, crewed by Sgts Jim Cammack and Doug Pye with Cpl Paul Baines framed in the doorway, was taken in the Camlough area on 26 August 2001 and shows the beautiful south Armagh landscape to its best effect.
KA Boyd

Army Aviation in Ulster

'South Armagh scenery 2.' The remoteness of the hilltop base in the background is well illustrated in this second view of 655 Squadron Lynx XZ641 flying over the south Armagh countryside on 26 August 2001.

KA Boyd

Lynx, loved by the pilots as fun to fly – a great old battlebus. 665 are proud of their more subtle skills, an urban rather than a rural presence, unobtrusively 'people watching'. 1 Flight is unique, with capabilities no other unit in the British Armed Forces can provide. REME are the technical masters – the organisers, the life blood of the entire operation.

The Joint Helicopter Force (Northern Ireland) (JHF(NI)) was established on 1 April 2000 (though, in effect, it had been functioning since the previous October). It is based at Aldergrove and its purpose is to co-ordinate and unify service flying in the province. The Officers' Mess is now joint service with the final function in the old army mess at Alexander Barracks being the Rhine Dinner on 21 March 2001, commemorating the anniversary of Operation Varsity, the airborne assault across the Rhine on 24 March 1945. The occasion was graced by the attendance of several veterans of the Glider Pilot Regiment. The link between 5 Regiment and the GPR is valued greatly on both sides. Being part of a tradition, having roots and a historical perspective are important to the young men of today, while the old soldiers take a 'grandfatherly' interest and remark proudly on the calibre and spirit of their successors. All enjoy the chance to discuss the hardware used today and yesterday. The mutual respect and comradeship which bridges the generations cannot be manufactured.

This spirit is maintained in the surroundings of the joint mess even down to the unique mechanised mess silverware which is a fine representation of the 'Jubilee class' express passenger steam locomotive *Bellerophon*. On Mess Nights tracks are laid around the tables and the engine pulls a train of trucks which can be used to convey messages and other items between the diners. The insignia of the Airborne Forces in World War Two was a representation of the mythological warrior of ancient Greece, Bellerophon, astride the winged horse, Pegasus.

The primary function of the Regimental Headquarters is command and this is exercised on the CO's behalf by the following personnel: the Second-in-Command (2IC),

Regimental Qualified Helicopter Instructor (RQHI). The position of RQHI is a coveted post within the AAC and is always held by a very experienced captain or major. He is responsible for the maintenance of flying standards and may be regarded as the air equivalent of the RSM. Along with his deputy, a Warrant Officer Class 1, the RQHI has a heavy workload. They bring all the pilots up to Category 3 NVG standard, which includes formation flying at night. They administer the mandatory yearly and six-monthly checks, the theatre qualifications and conversion to role training. In this last task they are assisted by the two QHIs with each squadron and 1 Flight's Qualified Flying Instructor (QFI), whose main jobs are squadron standards and training. The RQHI alone conducts the qualification tests for aircraft commander status. All the seven instructors in the Regiment are also available for line pilot duties as required.

Commanding Officers –
Northern Ireland Regiment AAC

1979 – 1981 Lieutenant Colonel DJ Ralls DFC, AAC
1981 – 1984 Lieutenant Colonel CJ Pickup AAC
1984 – 1986 Lieutenant Colonel KE Reid AAC
1986 – 1988 Lieutenant Colonel PDP McQueen AAC
1988 – 1990 Lieutenant Colonel MD Webb AAC
1990 – 1992 Lieutenant Colonel IP White AAC
1992 – 1993 Lieutenant Colonel D Husband OBE, AAC

5 Regiment AAC

1993 – 1994 Lieutenant Colonel D Husband OBE, AAC
1994 – 1996 Lieutenant Colonel RPD Folkes AAC
1996 – 1998 Lieutenant Colonel PC Roberts MBE, AAC
1998 – 2000 Lieutenant Colonel NJW Moss AAC
2000 – 2002 Lieutenant Colonel CHG Baulf MBE, AAC
2002 – 2004 Lieutenant Colonel D Venn AAC
2004 –   Lieutenant Colonel FG Budd MBE, AAC

15 September 1997 and Sgts John Sweeney and Pete Broadhead leave the 'garden' helipad at Bessbrook in 665 Squadron Gazelle ZA775.

KA Boyd

a senior major, who has a wide range of responsibilities including finance, logistics, infrastructure, equipment holdings, organisation, deployment, security and information technology. He in turn is supported by the Adjutant, a senior captain, and his assistant, who deal with matters pertaining to personnel, discipline and career management. The Regimental Sergeant Major has an important disciplinary function too, as well as being the Senior Warrant Officer and President of the Sergeants' Mess. The functions of the Training Officer and the Operations Officer, both captains, are explained by their titles. The Chief Clerk, normally a Staff Sergeant, heads the office staff.

The CO's regimental adviser on flying matters is the

1 Flight

This unit is the sole operator of fixed-wing aircraft in the AAC. It traces its ancestry back to February 1947 when 'C' Flight of 657 Squadron was retitled 1901 Flight. The aircraft flown were Hoverfly R-6 helicopters and

Army Aviation in Ulster

Auster AOP6s, firstly from Andover before moving to Middle Wallop in January 1948. The R-6s had little effective operational capability but gave the army valuable experience in the potential of the helicopter as it was developed further. In addition to AOP artillery direction, these experimental activities included photography (the first AOP6 modified for photography made its maiden flight, flown by Captain Moss, on 17 June 1947), radar trials, air/ground communications, fighter evasion (with Spitfires and Meteors) and comparative climb tests with the Auster (in which the Auster defeated the helicopter). The Hoverfly set an altitude record of its own on 14 July 1947 when KN842, in the hands of Captain Baker, reached a height of 8600 feet.

The Flight remained part of 657 Squadron until 1952, when it became part of 652 Squadron, based at Detmold in West Germany and equipped with four Auster AOP6 and one Auster T7. The unit history describes this time as follows:

> Life was dominated by training – training, first of all, as part of a British Army of the Rhine dedicated to intensive and almost continuous unit and formation training, and, secondly, flying and tactical training of a freedom surely unequalled in any place or at any time. Low, tactical flying and field landings were permitted almost everywhere in the British Zone of Germany.

In 1956 the Flight was re-equipped with the Auster AOP9. On the formation of the AAC in 1957, it was re-titled 1 Recce Flight and received its first Skeeter AOP12 on 20 December 1958. In January 1964, a further reorganisation resulted in the Flight becoming part of 655 Squadron and a change of designation to 1 Flight Army Air Corps. January 1967 saw the arrival of Sioux helicopters, followed the next year by Scouts. In August 1968 1 Flight was amalgamated with the Air Troops of 17/21 Lancers, the Queen's Dragoon Guards and 3 Royal Horse Artillery to form 1 Interim Squadron AAC at Detmold, which itself was renamed 661 Squadron in 1969. The title 1 Flight therefore lay dormant for the next twenty years until 1 October 1988, when the already existing Beaver Flight at Aldergrove was re-designated 1 Flight AAC.

A sad farewell to the reliable and distinctive Beavers was said some eight months later, the final flypast being made by XP769 and XP825 on 18 June 1989. The "wonderful whine of the radial nine" disappeared from Ulster skies after twenty years. They were accorded this

DHC Beaver XV272 taxies along runway 25 at Aldergrove in this undated shot. Does 'Operation Drake' on the aircraft date the view? Lough Neagh and an overbridge on the Lisburn–Antrim railway line can be seen beyond the threshold of runway 17.

R Burrows

5 Regiment, Army Air Corps

Britten Norman Islander AL1 ZG848 of 1 Flight Army Air Corps is pictured at RAF Aldergrove.

J Woods

affectionate valedictory tribute:

> No longer will the oil-covered aviator, smelling of AVGAS, be climbing on the wing to fill up the tip tanks. Nor will the illustrious pilot be looked at in complete astonishment at major airports all over Europe as they walk out to turn the prop before start.

Their role as the fixed-wing element of army flying was taken over by the Britten-Norman Islander, one of the most successful aircraft designed in Britain since the war, with over 1300 having been produced since 1965. The maiden flight was from Bembridge, Isle of Wight, on 13 June of that year and was flown by John Britten and Desmond Norman in G-ATCT. The first army Islander AL1, ZG846, arrived at Aldergrove on 10 March 1989, a flight of five aircraft being formed.

For a decade and more these versatile aircraft have performed a variety of roles in the province, and beyond, with quiet, unobtrusive efficiency. Its primary task, under the direction of the Reconnaissance, Intelligence and Geographic Centre (RIGC), is photoreconnaissance. A range of camera equipment is available to provide either high-level, low-level or oblique photography. Much of the work has been, and remains, sensitive as it is directly in support of the security forces on the ground. However the unique abilities of the aircraft have been used in support of the civil community in Northern Ireland and the rest of the UK. Much work is done on behalf of the Ordnance Survey and assistance has been given to several police forces looking for missing persons, while both HM Customs and Excise and the police have been helped in their searches for smugglers and drug runners. A few years ago, a photographic mission required 100 low level passes parallel with and across the runways at Heathrow Airport. So efficiently were they conducted, that not a single passenger flight had to be delayed or diverted.

The RIGC has been in business since 1973 as a tri-service and civilian unit. All its tasks are customer-generated and the need for its processing and associated keep it operational 24 hours a day, 365 days a year. As well as the Islanders, helicopters and high-flying RAF Canberras can be called upon for a variety of mapping tasks.

In the photographic role, the Islander is handled by a single pilot, while the aircrewman operates the camera control console and assists with the exact positioning of the aircraft. Satellite navigation has a high degree of accuracy and the radar altimeter is very useful in maintaining an exact height but for the best results on photographic runs, the aircrewman studies the ground through a clear view panel in the floor of the cabin, comparing what he sees with a map or photograph using the ever reliable 'Mark 1 eyeball'. The skill and expertise of the crew, as well as the flight plans supplied by the RIGC, have resulted in a 97% success rate for photo sorties. The aircraft is a very stable platform; it can carry a useful payload of bulky camera equipment, has a good endurance of more than four hours and is quite quiet, so promoting better community relations.

Secondary tasks include liaison flying, familiarisation flights, the carriage of senior officers, duty trips to Middle Wallop (taking two and a half hours rather than Chris Sherlock's epic five hours plus), the rapid delivery of important spares or equipment and compassionate cases. These last named are very important from the point of view of maintaining morale; support is given in this respect to all three services in Northern Ireland. Over the last few years, the Islanders have travelled widely throughout the UK and further afield to France, Germany and Norway. They have provided a very flexible and cost-effective asset and, as well as being able to use very short runways and simple prepared strips, they are fully airways-capable. The Flight Management System (FMS) and autopilot take much of the strain out of transit flying; they can fly through or (using their radar) around very poor weather or icing conditions. Their only limiting factor is that they are unpressurised and do not fly above 10,000 feet. A little heralded, but extremely useful, overseas deployment took place in early 1991 when a 1 Flight Islander flew to Saudi Arabia to undertake communications duties between HQ British Forces and the forward units in the desert. The same aircraft, ZG993, was also used later in a support role in the Balkans. In both cases, all the aircrew and indeed the groundcrew, had seen extensive service in Northern Ireland. There is no doubt that the operational experience gained there proved invaluable in these other theatres.

The complement of the flight allows for a QFI (Qualified Flying Instructor). Conversion training is carried out at Middle Wallop; in Northern Ireland the old

With Binevenagh in the background this can only be the former RAF aerodrome at Ballykelly, Co Londonderry. SSgt Andrew Corns makes a low level pass in 1 Flight Islander ZG844 on 1 June 1995.

Lt Col LJD Callow

RAF station at Ballykelly is used, as are the local airports. It is not, however, a posting that is suitable for a very inexperienced aviator, as much of the work involves single-pilot operation. It takes a certain level of confidence and knowledge to fly a small aircraft along the airways, in any weather, at any time of the day or night and then be able to adapt to the very different requirements of low-level photography. A further duty is giving assistance to the Air Support Unit of the PSNI, which is also located at Aldergrove and is equipped with a very similar aircraft.

All these tasks are undertaken by a very small but hard-working complement – six pilots, five aircrewman and two operations staff. In a normal month each pilot would be tasked to fly about 25 hours, though in the summer this can increase to up to 40 hours. The OC of the Flight can be either a major or a captain, the 2IC is a captain, while the other pilots are warrant officers or sergeants. There is a real pride shown in the versatility of the aircraft and in the vital nature of many of the tasks performed. Thoughts are now turning to the eventual replacement of the Islander and possible contenders might be the BN Defender 4000 and the Cessna Caravan.

Flight Commanders

Mar 79 – Jan 82	Major NPH Macauley RA
Jan 82 – May 83	Major NJ Law AFC, AAC
May 83 – May 85	Major NPH Macauley RA
May 85 – Dec 87	Major N O'Brien AAC
Dec 87 – Dec 89	Major GA Bacon RAEC
Dec 89 – Apr 90	Lieutenant L Henderson AAC
Apr 90 – Aug 92	Captain R Petrie AAC
Sept 92 – Jun 93	Captain NC Dann AAC
June 93 – Jul 94	Captain J Webber AAC
July 94 – Aug 95	Captain JD Wright AAC
Aug 95 – Oct 96	Captain IP Hall AAC
Oct 96 – July 97	Major AM Hudson AAC
July 97 – Apr 98	Captain ADC Maddock AAC
Apr 98 – Dec 00	Major DJ Willis AAC
Jan 01 – Mar 02	Captain CM Daly AAC
Mar 02 – May 04	Captain Steve Graham AAC
May 04 –	Major JM Thwaites AAC

Aircraft flown by 1 Flight and its predecessors from 1947
Hoverfly R6
Auster AOP6
Auster T7
Auster AOP9
Skeeter AOP12
Sioux AH1
Scout AH1
Beaver AL1
Islander AL1

655 Squadron

The story begins at Old Sarum airfield in Wiltshire in December 1942 with the formation of No 655 (AOP) Squadron, Royal Air Force. The main role of the Air Observation Post squadrons, of which there were 16, was to provide targeting and direction information to the artillery on the ground. Therefore, many AOP pilots were army gunnery officers, drawn from artillery regiments. 655's first CO was Major EB Ballard RA and a large proportion of his pilots were from 80th (The Scottish Horse) Medium Regiment, Royal Artillery. These officers continued to wear the bonnet and badge of their parent regiment. It was equipped with Mk I Austers and, after initial training, the new squadron moved to Gatwick in March 1943 in preparation for active duty, being re-equipped with Mk III Austers. Sadly, Major Ballard was killed whilst carrying out evasive tactics training and was replaced by Major DPD Oldman RA.

The squadron went overseas on 12 August 1943, embarking at Gourock for North Africa and arriving in Algiers a fortnight later. After further training it was ordered to join the Eighth Army in Italy. On 9 December the aircraft took off for Naples via Sicily. Its early experiences have been recorded as follows:

> 655's arrival in Italy did not go quite according to plan. The 16 Austers, shepherded by a Catalina flying boat, had flown from North Africa in stages. They were greeted by 12 Lockheed Lightning fighters which dived in formation to salute the squadron's landing. The pilots were further surprised and gratified to find that the courteous Americans had arranged a large reception committee. A senior American officer roared up in a jeep and asked if they were part of the fighter escort. One of

the pilots explained, with great politeness, that this was not the role in which the British used Austers; he went on with some enthusiasm to outline the nature of an AOP squadron's duties and was about to hint that a glass of beer would be appreciated, when the American burst out "The President of the USA is landing here in five minutes and if you do not get the hell out of here pretty damn quick, the fur will sure fly!"

The Squadron took the hint!

Spotting and reconnaissance duties commenced in December from a landing strip south of the River Sangro, despite the hazardous ground and flying conditions. Landing required an interesting technique:

> We sank down, for the mud was in splendid condition and the best way to land was to touch down with brakes hard on and skate, slither and slide to a standstill.

From January 1944, the six aircraft of 'A' Flight served alongside 'The Scottish Horse' during the Anzio landings and subsequent establishment of a bridgehead for the liberating forces. On the morning of the initial assault, visibility was down to about 100 yards and the aircraft flew, at times, only six feet above the water. One aircraft got lost in the fog and emerged to find itself over the enemy, just above the ground. Luckily a slow and low Auster was probably the last thing the Germans had expected to see, so he was able to make good his escape.

A close alliance was formed between the squadron and the regiment. The effectiveness of their co-operation may be judged from remarks made by the German commander, General von Zangen:

> The enemy artillery was frequently directed by air observation. With the aid of these aircraft, the enemy were able to kill off strong point after strongpoint with concentrated fire.

German Focke-Wulf Fw 190 and Messerschmitt Me 109 fighters attempted to shoot down the Austers which were bringing down such destructive artillery fire on the enemy positions.

The Squadron suffered its first active service casualty on 23 February, when Captain Dutton was shot down over Anzio and badly burned. 655 Squadron flew its Austers over the battlefields of Cassino, Rome, Florence, the Gothic Line, Senio, Po and Trieste with great gallantry throughout the long campaign along the Italian peninsula. Sometimes the methods used were somewhat unorthodox; on one occasion the pilot of an aircraft of 'C' Flight, registering a target on the 36th (US) Division front, was forced by bad weather to observe from a point out to sea behind the German lines, the only position from which he could obtain reasonable visibility. Though subjected

An Auster 'dug in' just short of Cassino, Italy.

Museum of Army Flying

throughout his sortie to intense fire from 88 mm artillery, he managed to return unharmed.

Following the capture of Rome in June 1944, there was time for a period of rest and also the opportunity to re-equip some of the squadron with Mk IV Austers. At this time the Squadron also learned of the award of its first decorations, two DFCs. Returning to operations, on 26 July the squadron was honoured by a visit from King George VI, who was flown by Auster to Malignano on his tour of the Italian front. During September high demands were made upon all personnel in the assault on the Gothic Line, not least because of the difficult terrain – suitable landing grounds were hard to find in the narrow, deep valleys north of Florence. In early December, command was assumed by Major PD Mackley DFC, RA but, only a few days later, he was killed in a flying accident. His place was taken by Major JS Stormonth-Darling RA. At this time a section of aircraft was detached from the main base at Castel del Rio to operate under the command of Land Forces, Adriatic in Yugoslavia for two months.

As the enemy resistance weakened, measures taken to encourage this included the dropping of propaganda leaflets from the Austers. By 30 April, the squadron had reached Mestre, near Venice. With the end of the war in Italy, duties were expanded to encompass information sorties to report on the movements of surrendered enemy forces and practice shoots with the Royal Navy, specifically the cruisers HMS *Orion* and HMS *Ajax*. Detached flights were based on the Italian-Yugoslav frontier, at Undine, Venice and in Milan. The final change of command was caused by the death of Major Stormonth-Darling, who was succeeded by Major TB Laird DFC, RA in August 1945.

By the time it disbanded on 31 August 1945, ten DFCs, three MBEs and eleven MIDs had been won but not without cost, as ten aircrew officers and one RAF airman were killed. When the hostilities were over the Corps Commander, General Harding, inspected the squadron and said:

> The country will not forget what many of you have endured, braved and achieved. Some of you here were very largely responsible for preventing the enemy from driving us into the sea at Anzio.

This profile shot of Scout XV124, callsign Army Air 863, was taken on 11 August 1976 as it flew into Sydenham; it was probably a 654 Squadron aircraft at this time. 655 Squadron's first tour of duty in Northern Ireland was carried out with Scout and Sioux helicopters, based at Long Kesh, from February to June 1973.

R. Burrows

Army Aviation in Ulster

Seventeen years later, in 1962, the squadron re-formed at Detmold in West Germany, as 655 Light Aircraft Squadron, Army Air Corps, equipped with Sud-Aviation Alouette II helicopters. Over the years, the links with 'The Scottish Horse' had been maintained, even though it had been amalgamated with other regiments. In 1971 permission was given to perpetuate the badge and the name of 'The Scottish Horse' by incorporating these into 655 Squadron's crest and informal title. After various changes of name, regiment, location and aircraft (which included, for a time, Sioux helicopters and Beaver liaison aircraft) the squadron received its present designation on 1 January 1973.

Its first tour of duty in Northern Ireland was carried out by Scout and Sioux helicopters, based at Long Kesh, from February to June 1973, the first of four spells there, the last ending in June 1979. Three Beavers, which at that time were still a part of the squadron, were based at Aldergrove between October 1973 and February 1974. In December 1979 the squadron moved from Topcliffe, in Yorkshire, to Omagh, County Tyrone, which was not the first visit of the squadron to this location. A brief tour at Omagh had been undertaken with five Scouts in the autumn of 1974. By 1979 it was equipped with Scout and Gazelle helicopters and was a part of the newly created Northern Ireland Regiment. A detached flight, flying Scouts, was also based at Aldergrove. The Scouts were replaced by Lynx AH1 helicopters and the squadron moved to Shackleton Barracks at Ballykelly, Co Londonderry in the summer of 1982. The Scout was a robust and well-loved helicopter but the Lynx was more modern, faster and with greater endurance. An unusual incident took place in December 1980 when Gazelle XX434 crashed (fortunately without serious injuries to the crew or passengers) after a passenger's bag became snagged on the helicopter's collective lever. Another Gazelle, XX400, suffered damage in south Armagh on 1 December 1982, when it struck some power cables.

In April 1984, a squadron Lynx, XZ665, carried out a most unusual 'aid to the civil community' task when it airlifted Grumman Wildcat V JV482 from Portmore Lough. The Wildcat was on the strength of No 882 Squadron, Fleet Air Arm and had taken off from Long Kesh airfield, on Christmas Eve 1944, on a training flight, flown by Sub Lieut (A) Peter Lock RNVR. After

655 Squadron Lynx XZ665 assisted in the recovery of Grumman Wildcat JV482 from Portmore Lough in April 1984.

Jack Woods

suffering engine failure, he was forced to ditch the aircraft into the lough, where it remained for the next 40 years. It now takes pride of place in the Ulster Aviation Society's Heritage Collection.

To return to less happy matters, the most serious incident to affect the squadron took place on 11 February 1990. Gazelle ZB687 was being flown on patrol close to the border near Clogher, in Co Tyrone when it was attacked by machine gun fire from the ground. A single 7.62mm round struck the machine, fracturing the main engine oil feed pipe. The pilot made an emergency landing and the three crew escaped from the wreckage with relatively minor injuries.

Over the years much effort has been devoted to countering the threat from the ground, terrorists having quickly realised the value of air assets to the security forces and, equally, the publicity that could be gained from shooting down a military aircraft. They proved to be innovative and skilful. In the early days, small arms fire was the main concern but higher calibre and automatic weapons posed a greater threat – working on the time-honoured basis of the more lead in the air the better. Rocket-propelled grenades (RPGs) and SAM 7 missiles considerably increased the terrorist's potential of achieving a 'spectacular'. Countermeasures included altering flying tactics, fitting armour plating to vulnerable areas, bolting on exhaust deflectors and developing advanced jammers. Naturally, a penalty had to be paid in operational flexibility, aircraft performance and electrical power required.

In 1991 the squadron decamped again, to Aldergrove, and would be much missed by two local schools – Glasvey Special School, Ballykelly and Greystone Hall School, Limavady – with which it had developed close relationships. On arrival the squadron became exclusively equipped with the Lynx and co-located with the rest of the Northern Ireland Regiment AAC.

September 1993 saw a very dangerous encounter with the Provisional IRA turn into a notable success. Two Lynx were escorting a Puma to Crossmaglen when they came under heavy and sustained fire from five different points, two of which were heavy machine guns mounted on flatbed lorries. As one of the vehicles moved off, a Lynx gave chase and the door gunner returned fire when the target was clear of the surrounding houses. When two more Lynx arrived, the vehicles were abandoned on a farm complex, the perpetrators managing to escape but eventually several vehicles, a number of weapons and hundreds of rounds of ammunition were captured. A few months later, in March, again while operating at Crossmaglen, a Lynx crew had a very lucky escape. They were dropping an underslung load at the base, when a mortar round smashed through the rotor disk and another took off the tail boom. The aircraft, a Lynx AH7, ZD275, ended up as a burnt-out wreck but the crew evacuated in the nick of time. The Airtrooper door gunner received a Mention

'Mutual Support 2'. Lynx XZ198 (nearest camera) and XZ667 over south Armagh.

Museum of Army Flying

in Dispatches for his bravery in helping the only serious casualty, a police constable of the RUC, to get out of the aircraft. (The Lynx AH7 had been introduced in 1991, its main advantages over the AH1 being improved avionics, reduced noise, better hover capability and more advanced composite rotor blades.)

Today, the squadron consists of four flights – 'A' and 'B' Flights are purely organisational designations, as the aircraft and duties are pooled, 'C' Flight uses the same resources for 'Special Duties' tasks and these three draw crewmen from the Air Door Gunners Flight. Seventeen Lynx AH7s are operated currently with nine aircraft being allocated on a daily basis for routine tasks. Two aircraft are allocated to south Armagh duties, two more for province-wide tasks, one is equipped with an airborne surveillance system, two aircraft are at readiness and two more are used for training and air tests. Up to four helicopters may therefore be in maintenance at any one time.

The standard roles of the Lynx have not really changed over the years. The re-supply of bases and outstations is still a priority in areas where road transport is less suitable – mail, rations, refuse and personnel form the normal cargo. Routine patrols are dropped off and quick reaction teams can be inserted speedily; surveillance and armed reconnaissance is still necessary, even in the current climate. The surveillance system used on the Lynx has improved over the years from the 'Heli-Tele' of the 1980s, to 'Chancellor' in the 1990s since replaced by the recently introduced 'Oxbow'. This system gives commanders on the ground a state of the art capability.

The major ports of call are Bessbrook, Enniskillen and Holywood, with Portadown, as an annual fixture, and Ballykelly – for training – being other regulars. Opportunities are also found for crews to fly to the mainland to take part in exercises and training.

The age range of the squadron pilots is from 25 to 45, while the door gunners are generally aged between 18 and 25. They are drawn from many arms of the service – Royal Artillery, Royal Engineers, Royal Logistics Corps and Royal Signals to name but a few – as well as direct entrants to the AAC. Most of those who have served in the province have gained great satisfaction from achieving an important task. It is interesting to reflect on their direct link with the early days of army aviation, some ninety years ago – operating not far above the ground, at speeds not that much over 120 knots and armed with a machine gun.

'Mutual Support 3.' As Lynx XZ662 lands on, XZ215 approaches over the east fence, while 1 Bn Welsh Guards soldiers, with an RUC officer, run from 72 Squadron 'Wessex 1' XR511 'L', crewed by Flt Lt Graham Jones, Flt Lt Jim Maginnis and Sgt Alan Swann. The date is 15 September 1997.

KA Boyd

Squadron OCs –

655 (AOP) Squadron RAF

Dec 42 – May 43	Major EB Ballard RA
Jun 43 – Dec 44	Major DPD Oldman RA
Dec 44	Major PD Mackley DFC, RA
Dec 44 – Jul 45	Major JS Stormonth-Darling RA
Aug 45	Major TB Laird RA

655 Light Aircraft Squadron AAC

Apr 62 – Jan 65	Major FL Russell MBE, DFC, AAC

HQ Army AV 4 Division

Jan 65 – Mar 65	Major FL Russell MBE, DFC, AAC
Mar 65 – Jul 67	Lieutenant Colonel R Wheen AAC
Jul 67 – Oct 69	Lieutenant Colonel AS Steptoe MBE, AAC

655 Aviation Squadron

Oct 69 – Jan 70	Major D Craig MBE, GM, AAC
Jan 70 – Jan 71	Lieutenant Colonel SMW Hickey AAC
Jan 71 – Jul 72	Lieutenant Colonel MG Badger DFC, AAC
Jul 72 – Dec 72	Lieutenant Colonel JL Dawson AAC

655 Squadron AAC

Jan 73 – Jan 74	Lieutenant Colonel JL Dawson AAC
Jan 74 – Sep 75	Major P Harrison AAC
Sep 75 – Feb 78	Major KE Reid AAC
Feb 78 – Mar 78	Major JRL Orde 15/19H
Mar 78 – Mar 79	Major RGL Pugh AAC
Mar 79 – Jun 81	Major The Lord Castlemaine AAC
Jun 81 – May 83	Major MA Perry AAC
May 83 – Dec 85	Major MS Buck AAC
Dec 85 – Apr 88	Major P Morrish AAC
Apr 88 – Dec 89	Major AJR Slessor AAC
Dec 89 – Sep 92	Major RH Tracy AAC
Sep 92 – Oct 94	Major PAW Edwards AAC
Oct 94 – Oct 96	Major CD Hogan AAC
Oct 96 – Feb 98	Major PJ Gibbs AAC
Feb 98 – Sep 98	Major IS Clements HLDRS
Sep 98 – Jul 00	Major EM Le Gresley AAC
Jul 00 – Sep 02	Major A Iceton AFC, AAC
Sep 02 –	Major G Owen AAC

Aircraft flown by 655 Squadron from 1942

- Auster I
- Auster III
- Auster IV
- Auster V
- Alouette II
- Sioux AH1
- Beaver AL1
- Scout AH1
- Gazelle AH1
- Lynx AH1
- Lynx AH7

The same day as the picture opposite 665 Squadron Lynx XZ662 and XZ215 head off from Bessbrook on another task.

KA Boyd

Army Aviation in Ulster

In this shot at Langford Lodge the troops are practising 'fast-roping' from a 655 Squadron Lynx.

RAF Aldergrove

'Mutual Support 4'. 655 Squadron Lynx XZ198 and 665 Squadron Gazelle ZB671 over south Armagh.

Museum of Army Flying

5 Regiment, Army Air Corps

Overlooked by Camlough Mountain and Bessbrook Mill, this scene is dominated by 655 Squadron Lynx. XZ649 leaves while XZ192 is shut down, together with XZ172 and XZ218. The date is 19 June 1996.

KA Boyd

Along with the other tasks, time must still found for routine training. Here we see a crewman firing a General Purpose machine gun from a 655 Squadron Lynx at Magilligan ranges.

SSgt DA Blackband

665 Squadron

On 22 January 1945, as the war in Europe was moving to its final climactic phase, the last but one AOP squadron was formed at Andover in Hampshire. It was a Canadian unit, destined to support the 1st Canadian Army. Major DR Ely RCA, who had served on AOP operations in the Italian campaign, was the squadron's first commanding officer. The first aircraft were delivered on 12 February. It was equipped with 16 Auster Vs (three flights of five each, with one attached to headquarters) and an Auster I for training. The time allowed for training was short and, sadly, during this period the squadron suffered its first casualty, when Captain Tony Eaton MC (the OC designate) was killed while on night flying practice, his Auster colliding with a Mosquito over the airfield. Captain NW Reilander was posted from 664 Squadron and promoted to Major, in order that he could take over from Major Ely, who was thereby released to organise the formation of the third Canadian squadron, No 666.

The squadron had a mix of ground personnel. According to Captain Cliff Ashfield RCA "Anything to do with the aeroplanes – (fitters and airframe 'erks', who looked after the Austers with enormous care) – was Royal Canadian Air Force, anything to do with the ground was army – cooks, drivers, signallers etc."

By the middle of March training had progressed sufficiently to allow the squadron to deploy independently to a new grass air strip at Oatlands Hill, near Stonehenge, and on 14 April Major Reilander and Captain Buchanan flew across the English Channel to begin the squadron's operational life. They were followed, within a few days, by the ground transport convoy and the rest of the aircraft to Airfield B77, near Gilze-Rijen in Holland, reputedly the second airfield largest in Europe. Instructions were given for the aircraft to deploy as follows: 'A' Flight to 2 Canadian Corps – to work with 1 Polish Armoured Division at Papenburg in Germany; 'B' Flight to be based in a farmyard near Dunkirk under 21 Army Group; 'C' Flight to Tilburg (where their base was a former asylum), as part of 1 Canadian Corps; while the Squadron HQ was to remain at Gilze for communications duties.

'C' Flight went into action first, on 27 April, with a counter-battery shoot conducted by Captain BRE Watch. The rest of the squadron engaged in active service in Holland, Germany and France over the next ten days, until 7 May, when Germany's unconditional surrender brought a swift end to 665's war. One of the tasks was to

This 1944 picture illustrates perfectly the role for which the Auster was intended – flying over a field battery and directing its fire.

Museum of Army Flying

fly to 10,000 feet (if the Auster could make it to that height) with meteorological instruments to carry out readings "while the ice tore off the fabric in little chunks" recalled Captain Ashfield. He also flew photographic sorties near the front line, steadily and at a fixed height. This allowed the developed photographs to be to be fitted into a constant-scale mosaic. A grid was superimposed over this, creating a map accurate enough for intelligence work and directing artillery fire. Captain Ray Irwin and Gunner Ray Knight of the Royal Canadian Artillery were paired together as pilot and spotter on several artillery shoots. The rear-seat spotter sat facing the tail and ran the stopwatch, communicating with the pilot by tapping him on the shoulder, confirming or correcting the fire of the guns below by means of the radio mounted in place of the front right-hand seat. The only armament carried was the pilot's 9mm pistol. Visibility from the Auster V was excellent – the pilot merely had to bank the aircraft and look through the perspex roof! Gunner Knight recalled 665 as being a very self-sufficient unit with very little formality or protocol. Apparently, at one point, a stock of fine Belgian crystal was 'liberated' and many toasts were made, with the glasses then being dashed into the fireplace.

While the surrender was taking place, Cliff Ashfield had one or two more adventures. Once he landed in a field in Holland to talk to some of the locals. It proved to be rather too well irrigated and the aircraft started to sink to the right. Luckily his sergeant had the presence of mind to jump out and support the starboard wing before clambering in again as the Auster picked up speed and departed – followed by "people in grey uniforms" whose intentions did not appear to be friendly. Several bullet holes were found in the Auster on its return to base. Later he visited a German-held airfield. They were reluctant to surrender to a junior officer and argued the point until Ashfield said "You don't have to surrender to us but tomorrow the 1st Polish Armoured Division will arrive and I don't think you will want to be here then."

On VE Day Captains Dinnich and Ashfield flew to England, along with two suitcases containing strong beverages, to sample, on behalf of the squadron, the atmosphere in Trafalgar Square during the celebrations. They flew out over the Hook of Holland and then across the North Sea ". . . at about 50 feet with spray on the windshield." On landing at a US airfield in East Anglia, they failed to discover a sober person on the base and continued on to London by train, where they bluffed their way into an expensive hotel. A completely successful sortie was reported. Major Reilander relinquished command on 13 June and was replaced by Captain Buchanan as acting OC. The squadron carried on with communications duties for a couple of months (Ray Irwin's flight was sent to the Allied HQ at Frankfurt to fly staff officers here and there) but was disbanded on 10 July, so terminating an initial incarnation of less than six months.

A generation was to pass before the squadron title was revived on 1 October 1969, when 19 Brigade Flight, 1 Royal Horse Artillery AOP Troop and 1 Prince of Wales Own Air Platoon were amalgamated to form 665 Aviation Squadron, at Munn Barracks, Colchester. The new unit was equipped with Scout and Sioux helicopters. Its first deployment in Northern Ireland was a four month tour at Aldergrove, beginning in June 1971, with a detachment of four Scouts, commanded by Captain Lambe. A further five visits were made to the province over the next six years – to Ballykelly, Sydenham, Omagh and Aldergrove again. It was retitled 665 Squadron Army Air Corps on 1 January 1973 . On 1 April 1978, it became 657 Squadron AAC. The second life of the squadron had lasted over eight years and less than a further eight years went by before it was reborn, at Aldergrove, on 12 March 1986. It became a permanent part of the Northern Ireland Regiment AAC and replaced the succession of squadrons on temporary roulement posting which had served in the Province previously. The squadron was trickle manned, with a proportion of the personnel being replaced regularly, as a concession to the high intensity nature of the work. At that stage it was equipped with both Gazelle and Lynx helicopters. In November 1987, as a seal on the squadron's status, a new badge, featuring a single maple leaf in honour of the squadron's Canadian origins, superimposed with a harp and the motto 'Providence', to signify its deployment in Northern Ireland, was conferred on it.

A baptism of fire came when, on 23 June 1988, Lynx XZ664 had to force-land in a field near Silverbridge, south Armagh, after coming under attack from the ground. One crewman was injured; the aircraft was later recovered by a Chinook heavy lift helicopter. Another

Army Aviation in Ulster

Cpl Julie Wyles, with Sgt Nigel Pitt as observer, takes ZB674 out of Bessbrook to return to Aldergrove on 13 January 2000.

KA Boyd

665 Squadron Gazelle ZB689 leaves Bessbrook en route to Aldergrove on 11 May 2000.

KA Boyd

Lynx, ZE380, was brought down in the same area on 13 February 1991; fortunately there were no serious injuries on that occasion.

Palace Barracks, at Holywood on the eastern edge of Belfast, was home to a flight of Gazelles. The main role of the 'City Flight' was to provide top cover for men on ground patrol. A young pilot commented:

> This is very different work from that in south Armagh because here we are doing a lot of high hover flying and slow orbits. We follow up incidents and can often be there in minutes. Navigation around the city is easy and when flying at night we can tell where we are by the pattern of the street lights.

An amusing story is told about a Gazelle preparing to take off from Palace Barracks. The aircraft commander suspended his HK53 rifle from the external boom of the helicopter, to leave his hands free as he completed his walkaround. His passenger, a fairly senior officer, gazed at the scenery, thinking happy thoughts. Checks completed, start up was initiated and clearance was given to depart. It is a feature of this base, that owing to the height of the nearby buildings and masts, the takeoff profile has to be vertical to gain sufficient altitude before nosing down into the transition to forward flight. All went smoothly for the first few seconds, until a message was received over the radio "Sir, I think you should return to base, you have scored a bullseye." Back on the ground, the pilot and his passenger were bemused until they discovered the HK53 with its muzzle embedded several inches into the tarmac, right in the middle of the painted H, having dropped off the boom from a height of 80 feet, as the Gazelle's nose went down. The moral of the story is, of course, obvious. Sadly the sport was not developed as an Olympic event!

In 1991, 665 became a Gazelle-only squadron; with 21 aircraft it was the largest in the AAC, and also the busiest, flying some 12,000 hours per year.

A very tragic accident involving a Squadron helicopter took place at Bessbrook on the night of 26/27 November 1992. As Gazelle ZB681 was taking off it collided with an incoming Puma HC1, XW233, of No 230 Squadron RAF. The Puma impacted into the perimeter security fence, while the Gazelle crash-landed close by. The two Gazelle crewmen escaped with injuries but all four personnel on board the Puma were killed.

Today the squadron has a special and distinct ethos. It provides the eye in the sky – cool and calm – assessing a situation and providing information to those on the ground.

The squadron HQ consists of the Officer Commanding (OC) – a Major, his 2IC – a senior Captain, the Squadron Sergeant Major – a Warrant Officer Class 2 (WO2), the Squadron Quarter Master Sergeant (SQMS), the squadron clerk and the Squadron Qualified Helicopter Instructor (SQHI), along with his deputy (usually a WO2) and a Staff Sergeant. They provide five additional pilots but by the very nature of their jobs, the OC, 2IC, SSM and QHIs have less time for routine duties.

The squadron is then divided into four flights. Two regular flights, 'A' and 'B' (plus 'G' Flight for special duties), pool the 21 Gazelles available for the 20 aircraft commanders and 12 pilots. All the aircraft commanders are, of course, pilots too. Usually it takes about six months for a new pilot of the rank of sergeant or above to progress to command. As is the case with the Lynx, once in the aircraft rank is largely immaterial – the commander, in the left-hand seat, is always in charge. During the course of normal duties, all aircraft commanders will undertake sorties as pilots in the right-hand seat to keep their flying skills in good order. Command of the fourth flight, the 'Ground Flight', is usually allocated to a newly arrived young lieutenant and provides a service to the entire regiment. Between 30 and 40 airtroopers and corporals, with a sergeant as the 2IC, are responsible for the ground handling of all the aircraft. This can be a very high pressure, busy environment in which to work. The shift pattern worked is 24 hours on and 24 hours off, and sometimes the duty crew will be working for all but three or four hours of this period. Moving aircraft in and out of the hangars and onto the dispersal area may not at first sound a challenging job but the value of the assets must be considered as well as the delicate and sensitive nature of much highly expensive equipment hanging off various booms or protruding from the fuselage. The operational nature of the tasks and the often inclement Northern Ireland weather adds to the pressure. Once the aircraft is on its spot, the ground crew are in charge of all refuelling and are present at all aircraft starts as safety cover. At the end of the tasking all non-technical care and maintenance is also in their hands.

Army Aviation in Ulster

Gazelle ZA774 features in this winter scene at Bessbrook on 30 December 2000. 72 Squadron Wessex XR506 'V' is the aircraft in the background.

KA Boyd

This is the observer's view from the left-hand seat of 'Gazelle 2' as the pilot, Sgt Stuart Pearce, brings XZ321, a Falklands War veteran, into a rural Forward Operating Base on 10 September 1999. Note the squadron number of the former 'tenants' painted on the ground.

KA Boyd

94

Framed against the terminus of the long-closed Bessbrook and Newry Tramway, 665 OC, Major RI Crosby, with Cpl Julie Wyles, as observer, lands Gazelle ZA774 in 'the well' at Bessbrook on 9 February 2000.

KA Boyd

The daily routine for the aircraft and aircrew is as follows: Gazelle 1 and Gazelle 2 are on call for liaison duties province-wide, including taking personnel to meetings or on tasks with a degree of urgency. Both aircraft are flown by an aircraft commander only. Gazelle 1's first priority is to be on call for the GOC (General Officer Commanding) but, if free, it can be made available to others eg for the author's familiarisation flight described later. Gazelles 3 to 7 are all twin crew with an aircraft commander and a pilot. The first three helicopters are allocated to 39, 3 and 8 Brigades respectively and are on call at the behest of the Brigade Commander. Gazelle 3 will spend its time at Palace Barracks or Aldergrove, Gazelle 4 at Bessbrook or Armagh and Gazelle 5 at either Londonderry, Omagh or Enniskillen. All three are equipped with Nitesun and BSS (as is Gazelle 6). The aircraft commander is in control of the mission equipment, which is mounted on external booms to the rear of the helicopter's fuselage. He has a screen and operating console, in front of him and to the left of the instrument panel. The extra weight of the mission equipment does not alter the flying characteristics of the Gazelle but it does slow it down and also has the effect of making it necessary to operate on a higher power setting.

Gazelle 6 is the 'night cab' and may be tasked to fly anywhere in the country during the hours of darkness, winter or summer. The crew fly with Night Vision Goggles (NVG) as standard. While these are a great aid to seeing in the dark, they are a strain to wear for any length of time, the heavy goggles having to be counterbalanced by a weight attached to the back of the flying helmet. The NVG has a downside as well, as peripheral vision and depth perception are reduced. Gazelle 7 complements Gazelle 6, providing the same capability but during the day.

As well as providing the manpower for these tasks, a pilot and an aircraft commander form the day's Duty Crew – they are at the call of the REME Light Aid Detachment (LAD) for ground running and air testing. Meanwhile the QHIs will be training and supervising check rides.

The Gazelle and Lynx aircrew perform separate and distinct functions which dovetail together. While the Lynx

Army Aviation in Ulster

665 Squadron Gazelle ZB671 dives away from an observation post on a remote south Armagh hilltop. These 'outposts' must be re-supplied from the air.

Museum of Army Flying

is a rough, tough noisy machine, which aims to move men and materials fast, the unobtrusive Gazelle acts in more of a stand-off role. The crew watch and monitor, they advise the commander on the ground and they cover everyone's back by looking beyond the periphery of an incident to see what might be building up in adjacent areas. The squadron is proud of its round-the-clock capability, as signified by the bat emblem which adorns the red and black flightsuit badge.

A certain amount of aid can also be given to the civil community, including casualty evacuation to hospital and, as happened recently, assisting in the apprehension of bank robbers. A Gazelle was called to observe the path of a getaway car and the crew was able, by giving skilful and accurate directions, to guide officers of the Police Service of Northern Ireland to the exact spot where they could best effect an arrest.

Typically a 665 Squadron pilot enjoys his work; the well-named, graceful and agile Gazelle is a delight to fly. It is a friendly and welcoming squadron where newcomers are readily accepted. The job requires a cool head and the ability to appreciate the bigger picture. A Gazelle pilot prides himself on being just a little more laid back than his more overtly dynamic Lynx colleagues – he is flying a little sports car rather than a hefty 4x4. So, perhaps, in years gone by, was there a similar rivalry, but underlying deep mutual respect, between light cavalrymen and those of the Heavy Brigade?

5 Regiment, Army Air Corps

Army Air Corps flying is a 24 hour a day operation as these two night images prove. The first shows Gazelle ZB685, piloted by Sgt Tim Woods with observer Capt George Cockton, as it approaches and lands at Armagh on 1 March 2000, while the second records Sgt Carl Bird and observer Sgt T O'Malley leaving Dungannon in Gazelle ZA730 on 30 November 1996.

KA Boyd

Squadron OCs –

665 (AOP) Squadron RAF

Jan 45 – Mar 45		Major DR Ely RCA
Mar 45 – Jun 45		Major NW Reilander RCA
Jun 45 – Jul 45		Captain WR Buchanan RCA

665 Aviation Squadron

Oct 69 –	1971	Major HHD Pullen R Ang
1971 –	1974	Major AB Bower PWO
1974 –	1976	Major RE Matthews DERR
1976 –	1977	Major RW England MBE, AAC
1977 –	1978	Major MA Orwin AAC

665 Squadron AAC

Mar 86 – Sept 88	Major MW Sample 15/19H
Oct 88 – Jan 90	Major RJ Lawes AAC
Jan 90 – Sept 90	Major SM Drennan MBE, DFC, AAC
Sept 90 – Dec 92	Major SRS Tanner AAC
Dec 92 – Mar 95	Major PJ Wright AAC
Jan 95 – Mar 97	Major BRE Butler AAC
Mar 97 – Mar 99	Major ACI Watts AAC
Mar 99 – Oct 01	Major RI Crosby AAC
Oct 01 – Sept 03	Major AAR Birkett AAC
Sept 03 –	Major PM Cook AAC

Aircraft flown by 665 Squadron from 1945

> Auster I
> Auster V
> Sioux AH1
> Scout AH1
> Lynx AH1
> Gazelle AH1
> Lynx AH7

5 Regt AAC Workshop REME

The Corps of Royal Electrical and Mechanical Engineers has maintained a presence at Aldergrove since the late 1950s and by the mid-1970s over 100 REME personnel were deployed in Ulster. Province-wide it supported the roulement squadrons with Light Aid Detachments (LADs). On the formation of the Northern Ireland Regiment, and the resultant centralisation of aviation support facilities there, the main REME unit, which had operated as 702 Mobile Support and Repair Detachment (MSRD) was retitled 70 Aircraft Workshop Detachment in December 1980. After a period as the Northern Ireland Regiment Aircraft Workshop, it assumed its present title in 1993 with the creation of 5 Regiment.

REME's tasks can be divided into five main areas: daily servicing, scheduled maintenance, unscheduled repairs, general modifications and alterations to the basic aircraft fit, which are specific to the role in Northern Ireland.

Daily servicing is a constant, relatively simple task – keeping the right number of aircraft available to fulfil the operational and training requirements of the regiment. Scheduled maintenance follows a service interval pattern in much the same way as a family car, but is based on flying hours rather than miles. The time involved can vary, depending on what is found to need rectification, but on average, a 25 hour check will take an hour or two, while 21 days are set aside for an 800 hour service on a Gazelle. These times are significantly lower than on the mainland. This is because of the operational nature of the task and the priority accorded to it. The workshop is scaled for 100% of its manning complement, rather than the usual norm of 60–70% in England. Spares support is given a high priority, too. A 24 hour shift system is worked and as the aircraft do not deploy on exercises (they are too busy), there is no requirement to maintain exercise kit or vehicles, nor are the craftsmen/technicians tasked for guard duties as they would be elsewhere. Unscheduled repairs can be as complex as changing the gearbox, engine or tailboom; this comes under the heading of 2nd Line Maintenance, as does any work of greater complexity than routine tasks. Even deeper scheduled maintenance (at the 800 hours interval and above for the Lynx and 1600 hours and above for the Gazelle) is carried out at Middle Wallop, while 3rd Line Tasks are the responsibilty of the Royal Navy, at Fleetlands, for all service helicopters.

The basic REME rank is the Craftsman, which equates to an Airtrooper. As well as promotion to NCO and beyond, the Craftsman progresses from Class III to Class II as his experience and knowledge increases. The majority of technicians come out of training as Lance Corporals. They all arrive in Northern Ireland qualified as Class II, being referred to as 'UTs' (Under Training) for about 12 weeks, while they gain sufficient experience to be fully fledged Class II technicians; at Class I level the work is of a more supervisory nature. At the hub of the action is the duty Crew Chief of each LAD shift (there is a separate one for each squadron). This sergeant is the first point of contact for aircrew reporting defects or seeking information on serviceability. It can be a very pressured environment, allocating priorities to tasks and scheduling work. It requires fine judgement, experience and the ability to cope with demands within a tight timescale. 1st Line servicing is the prime function of the LAD, a small, highly trained crew of between 18 and 25 aircraft and avionics technicians, organised into two shifts to give round-the-clock cover. 2nd line servicing has been added to the LAD's functions with an enhancement of personnel to allow for this. 665 LAD also encompasses 1 Flight's LAD.

Management functions begin at Staff Sergeant (Artificer) and Warrant Officer level, covering quality control and the keeping of all the vitally necessary technical logs. The senior warrant officer, the Artificer Sergeant Major (ASM), will have considerable experience, carry a great deal of authority and is very much the OC's right-hand man. The LAD OC, a captain, is supported by an Artificer Quartermaster Sergeant (AQMS).

Commissioned officers, as middle management, can see the bigger picture, take higher level engineering decisions and look after the welfare and careers of the soldiers. They also act as a safety valve and filter between the demands of the flying task and the practical feasibility of fulfilling it technically and safely. A Major is in command, with a Captain in charge of each LAD and the Workshop Main, covering such areas as ground support equipment, the toolstore, the Armourer and 133 Aviation Support Unit RLC. This last named is a small, self-contained, but very important, body of Royal Logistics Corps' personnel. They administer a range of thousands of spares rising, in value from a few pence to half a million pounds. The REME and RLC soldiers, though taking a great pride in their parent Corps, feel very much a part of 5 Regiment.

The lines of communication between aviators and

Army Air Corps aircraft are maintained to exacting standards. Here, on 6 September 2000, 665 Squadron Gazelle XX405 is seen reduced to component form during an 800 hour 'service'.

KA Boyd

655 Lynx XZ655 and 1 Flight Islander ZG844 undergo similar maintenance schedules to the Gazelle in the 5 Regiment hangar.
KA Boyd

support staff are direct and specific and the organisation is well-structured, logical and sensible. REME is justly proud of its ability to organise efficiently and make a complex technical operation (looking after more than 40 aircraft) run smoothly; teamwork and co-operation are essential. REME feel that having a different cap badge and management chain is a strength, as line managers will support decisions made on a sound technical basis. However, as with the rest of the regiment, a 'can do' spirit prevails. If it is humanly possible to have an aircraft fully ready for service, it will be there, on time and fit for the task. REME's greatest strength is the organisational ability of its personnel – identifying the key elements and sequences of a task, making complex jobs and schedules manageable. Perhaps the best example of this is that seemingly mundane location, the toolstore. It is beautifully organised, tally marked and colour coded – a place for everything and everything in its place and to hand when required. However, lest it be thought that REME is entirely without blemish, the following story should be told. One day a visiting General was inspecting the workshop and saw some men hard at work rubbing down rotor blades. The OC explained that the weight and balance of each blade was crucial. The General, wishing to show an intelligent interest, enquired as to the exact weight of a blade. The OC asked the ASM, the ASM tried not to look as blank as the OC. In the background a voice interjected "A blade weighs 82 pounds, Sir". The general congratulated the RSM, expressed admiration for his technical knowledge and asked how he had acquired it. The RSM replied "It's printed on the side of the blade, Sir."

Turning to the aircraft, the Gazelle is well-regarded by the craftsmen and artificers. It is a well-proven, very reliable aircraft and requires very little in the way of unscheduled maintenance, which speaks volumes for a type which has been in service in Ulster for twenty-five years. The design is not complex; it is a simple airframe, allied to a good engine and gearbox. The conflict in the Falklands revealed certain weaknesses on the battlefield but in Northern Ireland it has been a most worthy successor to the Sioux.

The Lynx poses a somewhat greater challenge. It is a rugged machine, with plenty of character and has proved to be a very versatile workhorse. It can, however, be rather temperamental from a maintainer's viewpoint. It thrives on hard work but does not appreciate long periods standing still. The 655 Squadron LAD is generally recognised as the busiest in REME. The ratio of flying hours to servicing hours has always been much higher for the Lynx than the Gazelle.

1 Flight LAD is a small, very specialised unit; being the Staff Sergeant in charge is regarded as a plum posting, as its gives responsibility and a certain amount of independence. Maintaining the Islander is generally a pleasant task and something less of an art form than working on the Beaver.

Workshop OCs

Oct 93 – Mar 95	Major PD Phillips REME
Mar 95 – Jan 97	Major MA Armstrong REME
Jan 97 – Aug 99	Major J Power REME
Aug 99 – Aug 01	Major SP Fitzgibbon REME
Aug 01 – Aug 03	Major JP Foster REME
Aug 03 –	Major DJ Eastman REME

Part 4: Flying with 5 Regiment AAC

1 Flight

With over 10000 hours in his logbook and 38 years of army service behind him, Warrant Officer Chris Sherlock was one of the most experienced pilots flying with the Army Air Corps. It was therefore a great pleasure and privilege to have the opportunity to fly with him in one of the four Britten-Norman Islander AL 1s of 1 Flight, stationed at RAF Aldergrove.

The Islanders have been in service with 1 Flight since 1989, when they replaced the rugged and reliable DHC-2 Beavers, which had been in the province for the previous 20 years.

The main task of 1 Flight is photographic reconnaissance in support of the Security Forces. These duties require very accurate flying at low and medium levels. The Islander has proved an excellent camera platform, being both manoeuvrable and stable, has a good endurance and can carry the full range of equipment necessary. Responsibility for deciding on the precise nature of each job lies with the Reconnaissance, Intelligence and Geographic Centre (RIGC), which is also located at Aldergrove. As mentioned earlier in the book this is a 24 hour, 7 days a week, 365 days a year operation, so an aircraft and crew has to be available at all times. The RIGC supplies the crew with a full briefing as to the exact nature of the task and provides detailed maps of the area which needs to be covered. On these maps the parameters of the photographic runs are plotted.

On being detailed for a sortie, the pilot and crewman collect their helmets, lifejackets and gloves and make their way to the aircraft. The pilot occupies the left-hand seat, with the crewman beside. However, the right-hand seat can slide fully backwards into the cabin to allow the crewman access to the particular cameras fitted for the mission and their control panel on the port forward sidewall of the cabin. No other seating can be fitted in this configuration, as the camera equipment is heavy and takes up a lot of room. My flight was to be a simulated mission, undertaken in ZG844, which had seats installed in the back and is normally used for the Islanders' important, secondary, role of transport and liaison.

As Chris carried out the customary walkaround and visual inspection of the aircraft's exterior, there was time to have a look at the Islander's flight instrumentation. It is fully airways capable and has not only an excellent autopilot (a feature which the otherwise admirable Beaver lacked) but also satellite navigation in the shape of a GPS and a flight management computer, or FMS. It was therefore a very simple matter for Chris, once he had brought the electrical system to life, to programme the FMS with our route to the 'target' area with waypoint details.

The start-up procedure is uncomplicated and the two Allison 320 shp turboprops were swiftly coaxed into noisy life. The ground handler was waved away and Chris asked Air Traffic Control (ATC) in the main Belfast International tower for permission to taxi, using the regular callsign Merlin. Clearance was given and Merlin 452 rumbled past the ranks of 655 Squadron Lynx and 665 Squadron Gazelles. Over to our right, a Gazelle was asking ATC for permission to conduct some local hovering practice, while an incoming Lynx passed across Runway 07/25 as we taxied onto it. The Islander is justly renowned for its exceptional short takeoff performance and I was not disappointed by our rapid departure, which used up only a few of the 9000 feet available. After clearing the circuit, we turned onto a heading of 319 degrees, towards Toomebridge and across the watery expanse of Lough Neagh, which was looking particularly leaden and chilly in the weak winter sunshine. The air was calm, with scattered clouds ahead and low lying mist to the right, around Randalstown. We climbed to 2000 feet and levelled out, continuing at the normal cruising speed of 150 kts. Over Toomebridge it was apparent that the heavy autumnal rains had left a legacy of flooding in the Bann valley. A normal photographic mission takes in the region of an hour and that was what had been planned on this occasion to give a flavour of a typical tasking. In the course of the average month, each pilot in the flight flies about 25 hours, though this can increase to 40 hours in the summer.

Nearing the target area, Chris, changed to the large scale map provided by the RIGC, which showed woods and farmland, with thick black lines delineating the photographic runs. We descended, reducing speed and increasing the engine revolutions. Chris flew a wide circuit, checking for pylons, high ground or other obstructions. Then, satisfied that he could carry out the mission within the demanding limits of accuracy required, he adjusted the radar altimeter and descended to the set height. We curved around quite steeply to start the first run and hit the entry point exactly. On a real sortie the crewman would have been staring through a clearview panel in the cabin floor to assist the pilot. The job requires skilled teamwork and absolute confidence in each other, something which only comes from experience and practice. Evidence that 1 Flight have the necessary skills in abundance is that fact that the success rate for jobs completed stands at 97%.

As we banked and turned onto the run, the feeling was akin to being driven in a high-performance car, perhaps a Jaguar in the Le Mans 24 Hour, as we powered over the trees and hedgerows. The Islander may not be quite as manoeuvrable or have the ultra-low speed capability of the Beaver but it can still perform very niftily, with that comfortable feeling of having plenty of power to spare. After we had climbed to 2000 feet again, Chris gave a little demonstration of the aircraft's agility, with some very tight wingtip turns.

We finished the trip with a cruise along the north coast for some very pleasant sightseeing – watching the

This is the view from 1 Flight Islander ZG993 on final approach to an RAF base 'somewhere in southern England'; Major George Bacon (left) and Cpl (now Sgt) 'Jono' Johnson are at the controls.

KA Boyd

Army Aviation in Ulster

waves crashing in on Blackrock beach and against the dark basalt columns of the Giant's Causeway.

Coming across Lough Neagh again, Aldergrove's secondary runway, 17/35, showed up very clearly in the distance as a long, black strip on a grey day. The sun had gone, the clouds were drawing in but the visibility was still reasonable. We joined the circuit for a landing on 25 but in order to save wear and tear on the tyres, Chris extended his short finals for a low-level pass along the runway landing much closer to the turn off before taxying back to shut down. It had been a thoroughly enjoyable experience in the hands of a highly professional and completely relaxed aviator.

Communications and liaison work is another important part of 1 Flight's routine – carrying personnel, dispatches and urgent spares. The Islander is equally at home flying at 9000 feet – where the thoughtfully provided car rugs are a boon for the passenger, as the aircraft is a little draughty – or taking the scenic route at 2000 feet. Alex Boyd and I were invited to accompany ZG748 on a typical journey to AAC HQ at Middle Wallop in Hampshire, via the Defence Helicopter School at RAF Shawbury, which is not far from Shrewsbury in Shropshire. Our pilot was the Flight's 2/IC, Captain Steve Graham, while his aircrewman was Sergeant Nick Parish – who featured in the 2001 edition of the AAC Journal when crewing an Islander on a delivery flight from the UK to Belize.

Our first sector from Aldergrove to Shawbury took an hour and a half at 9000 feet and a steady 135 kts. Time on the ground there was a nifty five minutes, allowing our third passenger to disembark. It was VFR thereafter all the way, over the English countryside at 2000 feet and 145 kts – past Gloucester, Lyneham, Andover and on to Wallop. Some highlights of the hour long trip included counting the 29 Hercules on the ground at Lyneham and seeing a smart black painted Hawk, zipping along below at 500 feet, taking swift evasive action as a microlight appeared out of the haze. Teamwork between the pilot and aircrewman was essential, two pairs of eyes keeping a very good lookout. Soon we were in the circuit above the wide grassy expanse of Middle Wallop, looking down on the menacing shape of some new Apaches, the yellow Fireflies and the black and yellow Squirrels.

Our tasks for the day were to meet with the staff of the Museum of Army Flying and to talk to some of the more experienced personnel in the training squadron about their memories of the days of Sioux, Scout and Beaver in Ulster. There was also a chance to have a close look at the marvellous old aircraft that comprise the Army Air Corps Historic Flight.

By mid-afternoon it was time to depart as we had to be at Shawbury before it closed for the day at 5pm. Once more we rumbled along runway 08/26; it was poignant to

Middle Wallop gate guardian, Westland Scout AH1 XT638, today fulfils a very different role to that of it in the view on page 50.

KA Boyd

104

think of the Spitfires, Hurricanes, Blenheims, Beaufighters and Mustangs using the same strip 60 years before. We enjoyed another link to a past era, as it was hands-on, map and compass flying all the way to Shawbury, again at 2000 feet. More microlights and Squirrels could be seen below as we retraced our path over crop circles and villages enclosed by ancient earthworks. The teamwork between Steve and Nick was once more apparent, the aircrewman with the map on his knee pointing out features to assist the pilot in adjusting our heading.

This time the record for length of time on the ground at Shawbury was reduced to only three minutes. Village cricketers near Shrewsbury stood out like white dots on the green and in a huge quarry near Wrexham the massive bulldozers and diggers looked like Tonka toys. Crossing the coast between Rhyl and Birkenhead we climbed to 3000 feet and tracked round the edge of a storm cloud, painted yellow on the weather radar. The car rugs came in handy, again, as in moist cloud the Islander is not completely waterproof. The rain had acted to clear the air and on approaching the Isle of Man the greens and browns of the fields stood out in sharp relief. Landing at Aldergrove was accomplished at 17.55 after a journey of over 600 miles in just on five flying hours – all in a day's work for 1 Flight.

655 Squadron

The Westland Lynx AH7 was introduced into AAC service from 1988. Most were the earlier AH1 airframes upgraded to the later standard, so the basic aircraft are mostly over 20 years old. It is a functional looking, rugged helicopter but due primarily to the advanced technology of the rotor blades is both fast and manoeuvrable. The two Rolls Royce Gem turboshafts provide a good reserve of power for all the tactical situations likely to be experienced in the province. Unusually for a helicopter, the handling pilot sits on the left, while the mission commander occupies the right-hand seat and, as noted earlier, command is a function of experience rather than of rank. 655 Squadron has more than 30 pilots of all ranks from corporal to captain. The task of mission commander may be undertaken by any pilot. It is not unusual for an experienced sergeant to be in charge with a captain, in the early months of his tour, as the handling pilot. In the air, rank is almost irrelevant; respect is given and military

The Army Air Corps Memorial at the entrance to their Headquarters at Middle Wallop.

KA Boyd

protocols are observed but for the team to be effective, professionalism rather than deference is the key. On my flight both pilots were sergeants but with more than two years flying with the squadron as compared to less than two months, there was no doubt that the right-hand seat would be taken by Dean Jobson, while Gary Leigh concentrated on the flying. The workload in the principal area of operations, south Armagh, is quite high. The handling pilot concentrates on flying the helicopter in conditions that can often be quite challenging given the often marginal weather in hilly terrain. He also deals with Air Traffic Control communications. Deconfliction in respect of other aircraft in this relatively small area is of major importance. The mission commander is free to concentrate on the overall direction of the task, tactical communications on the secure radio nets and giving advice on the particular problems posed by any of the landing sites.

The avionics fitted to the Lynx have been updated over the years to the extent of replacing TANS by GPS, though not on all machines as yet. One of the most useful features is the Automatic Flight Control System (ACFS) which stabilises the aircraft in yaw and pitch and can be used to set height and heading, principally on long transit flights. In south Armagh all the flying is manual and most of the navigation is carried out by the mission commander with his set of detailed maps.

Before proceeding onto the flight line to board XZ205, there was a considerable amount of organisational routine to follow. The daily tasks are now allotted by JHF(NI) but there is still much work to be done in the regimental and squadron operations and planning rooms. The 5 Regiment planning room contains all the necessary maps which may be drawn out as required and also the armoury in which the weapons and ammunition are stored. The operations room has detailed, up to date, presentations of all the information needed to fly safely and within the rules; also stored there are the secure radios and the various forms that have to be completed. The squadron operations room is where the daily schedule is plotted, individual flight plans are prepared and much coffee is consumed. Last but not least a visit is made to the Safety Equipment Section, which is manned by embedded RAF personnel, who are responsible for the issue and servicing of such item as helmets, life jackets, life rafts, immersion suits and night vision goggles.

On leaving the building and before walking out to the aircraft, flying helmets have to be put on and this had the effect of limiting any explanatory talk until we were hooked up to the intercom. It was therefore a good time to stand back and take a few photographs as the three crew members quietly and efficiently performed their pre-flight walkaround and checks. The third crewman was Airtrooper Dan Moran, who concentrated on mounting and loading the General Purpose Machine Gun (GPMG), while the two pilots removed covers, carefully examined the rotorhead and powered up the systems. Luckily, as this was a training sortie, I did not have to share the cabin of Lynx 10 with 6–8 fully equipped troops. For all its many virtues, the back end of a Lynx can only be described as less than roomy, somewhat basic and rather spartan as regards creature comforts.

Start up was a swift and simple business; last man in was the air gunner, who kept a good look out all round through the open door as we lifted off and swiftly hover-taxied away. Under the control of Aldergrove Tower, we rose quickly to 1500 feet and flew south along the shores of Lough Neagh, across Portmore Lough, the waters of which were glistening in the weak winter sunshine.

As we turned west to follow the line of the M1, we spotted a light aircraft below at no more than 100 feet, using the motorway to navigate. Going south again and passing between Portadown and Lurgan (a regular haunt of the squadron in July – Drumcree time), we were advised to watch out for a JetRanger on an electricity pylon survey task and sure enough one swam into view, going from right to left across our path. In its northern half, County Armagh is quite flat and fertile. Apple growing is a feature and in spring the orchard county is very attractive.

Travelling south, the land quickly becomes much more hilly with scattered small mixed farms and market towns dotting the landscape. The most distinctive features are the bleak brown mass of Slieve Gullion and its attendant hill-tops spread around. It is on these that the remote little army bases with their high watchtowers and landing pads are situated. Some of the rust-coloured pads look barely big enough to accommodate a helicopter. Replenishing these sites and landing patrols into fields are 655 Squadron's bread and butter. This is where the skill and expertise of the mission commander comes into its own, advising on the best means of landing a machine on a very limited space, on a hill-top, in all weathers, with the winds eddying around to trap the unwary. Additionally, he has to pinpoint, with absolute accuracy, a field looking similar to hundreds of others in which troops are to be picked up or inserted. In all landings and takeoffs the role of the air door gunner is vital. His prime responsibilty is the security of the aircraft, not only offering defensive protection with the GPMG but also ensuring that there are no obstructions or other hazards. He (or indeed she – as all aircrew can be men or women) also has to ensure the safe loading and unloading of soldiers or stores. Moreover, the aircrewman is team-medic trained and is therefore able to provide very valuable assistance in a casualty evacuation.

Flying with 5 Regiment AAC

These two scenes at Bessbrook date from the late 1980s/early 90s and feature 7 Squadron Chinook ZA704 'J'. The upper view shows a 655 Squadron Lynx climbing away while the Chinook lands outside the fence.

Museum of Army Flying

655 Squadron Lynx XZ667 departs as 7 Squadron Chinook ZA704 'J' prepares to lift an underslung load.

Museum of Army Flying

107

On top of this, when TV equipment is carried, this can also be operated by the crew in the back. It can be seen, therefore, that the aircrewman carries considerable responsibilities for his rank and only the most promising candidates are selected for air door gunner duties. It is entirely possible that in time they can progress to pilot training.

Having surveyed several of the hill-top bases. it was time to call in at the nerve centre of the local operation, Bessbrook Mill. Landing at this location is exciting; the descent profile is rapid and steep, followed by a hedge-hopping final run in, to pop over the boundary fence and land on the very confined space onto which up to six helicopters can be squeezed. We were on the ground for some 3–4 minutes, in which time a Puma departed and we took on fuel. Meanwhile, we heard that Lynx 5 and 6 were on their way.

The old mill at Bessbrook is a byword in rotary-wing circles which was, in the past, the busiest heliport in the world. It has performed a vital role over the years but could not be described as picturesque or even homely; grey, monolithic and severely functional would be more apt adjectives. It lies eight miles from the closest part of the border with the Irish Republic, 40 miles southwest of Belfast and 64 miles north of Dublin. It has a most unusual connection with the early days of aviation, as in the first decades of the 20th century Bessbrook Mill established a reputation for producing the finest quality aeroplane linen. Many fabric-covered biplanes of the Royal Flying Corps went to France clad in doped linen from the mill. Indeed the Austers of the Second World War may also have been similarly furnished.

Returning to Aldergrove after a thoroughly fascinating afternoon there was the opportunity to experience another of the unexpected hazards that a helicopter pilot may encounter. Near Banbridge, a little yellow microlight swam past, perfectly legally in uncontrolled airspace, not in radio contact with anyone, oblivious to the world.

665 Squadron

When WO2 Kev Bridge suggested that we should go and visit 'Baldrick', it sounded intriguing Having been issued with my Mk 15 flying helmet and a size 10 flying suit, I quickly put these on and followed the warrant officer across the dispersal area to where Gazelle AH1 XZ339 was lurking in the long grass on the far side. There could be no doubt that Kev was a Gazelle man through and through. He had in excess of 3500 hours on type and was the squadron's QHI. The prototype SA340 first flew in 1967 and was designed by the French manufacturer, Sud Aviation, as a replacement for the Alouette II. Following the the same year's inter-governmental agreement on helicopter production, the developed Gazelle was also manufactured by Westland for British military use. For its class it has an excellent rate of climb and top speed. It has given the British Army more than a quarter of a century of front-line service. I was soon to find out why it is so well-loved by all who have flown the aircraft.

On reaching XZ339, Kev began his walkaround with a practised but still careful eye, checking that all was as it should be and that there were no hatches insecure or leakages of fluid. To look at, the Gazelle is a very neat and attractive helicopter. Everything has the aspect of being in proportion – from the streamlined, 'teardrop' cockpit canopy to the Turbomeca Astazou turboshaft mounted to the rear of the cabin and the enclosed fenestron tail fan. As I climbed into the very comfortable, sheepskin padded left-hand seat, the next great plus feature was readily apparent – the splendid all-round view. Kev had completed his external checks and settling down into the right-hand seat, he buckled the five-point harness and began the pre-start up procedure. Having turned on the electrical power, he checked the switches, warning lights and dials on the instrument housing and then the roof mounted rotor brake, throttle and emergency fuel cut off. Here his well-schooled eye and hand stopped, as he noticed that the locking wire on this last named lever had come adrift – possibly cut by the rotor brake handle. A swift radio call from Gazelle 1 to the Ops Room brought a cheerful REME sergeant and his mate out for a stroll in the sunshine and we were soon back to A1 condition. Having listened to the recorded airfield advisory service (ATIS) on 128.2 MHz, Kev changed to the Aldergrove Ground Control frequency on 127.75 MHz and requested start-up, this time using the call-sign Hawk 410. This was duly given and the boost pump was depressed to bring fuel into the system. The start and ignition switch brought the engine whistling into life and we watched the dials as the temperatures and voltage wound up. The Global

665 Squadron Gazelle XZ339 is refuelled at Palace Barracks, Holywood, as XX370 departs on 24 July 2001.

Guy Warner

Positioning System (GPS) and radar altimeter were then turned on as we waited. All looked good, so the upper red strobe was flashed to indicate to the waiting handler (standing in the long grass, with protective goggles, ear defenders on and a portable fire extinguisher to hand, just in case) that we were ready to engage the rotor blades. Kev slipped the rotor brake and carefully advanced the throttle. As the rotor speed and engine revolutions crept up to the same point on the dial, the handler came forward carefully and ducking below the whirring blades, completed a final external safety check. Gazelle 1 was then announced on the tactical radios as being ready to go. With engine and rotor revolutions stabilised, departure was requested from the tower on 118.3 MHz. Clearance being given, Kev raised the collective gently with his left-hand and keeping the helicopter in balance with subtle inputs of the cyclic and yaw pedals, rose imperceptibly into the hover. We turned 360 degrees to make sure no errant personnel or aircraft were in the way and picking up speed and height, departed over the grass, parallel to runway 17/35. It was time to go and see the mysterious 'Baldrick'.

Rising to 2000 feet, Belfast Lough could be seen glittering in the distance and as we passed between Divis and Black Mountain, the city came into view. There would be time to examine the Gazelle's habitual operating environment later. Crossing over harbour and the smart new terminal at Belfast City Airport, we reduced height and turned east until we were orbiting Palace Barracks, the army base at Holywood on the eastern edge of the city. Having advised 'Baldrick' on the radio that we were going to pay him a visit, Kev opted for a tactical approach. He stood the Gazelle on its nose to gain speed, so making a steep and rapid descent onto the pad. An Airtrooper driving a fuel bowser approached as the rotors wound down. This was 'Baldrick', so called because he was the duty jack of all trades. For a period of a week, one of the Ground Flight is based at Palace Barracks. He is on-call 24 hours a day to handle and refuel all incoming helicopters, to man the radio and to answer the telephone in the crew room. We were the sixth visitor that day, at a busy time it could be three or four times this. Our 'Baldrick' was

Airtrooper Adrian Monteith, aged 19, and this was his first detachment. Again it was apparent, as was the case with the air door gunners of the Lynx squadron, that the AAC believe in giving responsibility and trust early to test the mettle of their high quality recruits.

Gazelle 3 was just leaving so Kev suggested that we would meet with him later over the city. As we had a cup of coffee in the crew quarters, which provides comfortable living, cooking and sleeping space for three, I asked Kev how long it would take him to be in the air if called urgently to an emergency. He replied that on the night of the bomb at the North Howard Street Mill, the time from this crew room to being in position over the mill was three minutes.

We took to the air again to have a look at a typical role for 665 Squadron. We were soon hovering over the city, laid out like a 3-D model below. With the familiarity engendered by many hours spent flying over Belfast by day and night in all weathers, Kev was able to point out all the familiar landmarks – the City Hall, Queen's University, Stormont, the City Hospital and also the locations sadly made notorious over far too many years – the Shankill Road, Crumlin Road Prison, the New Lodge, the yellow wall that constituted the peace line, Andersonstown, with its fortresslike police station, Poleglass. At random he picked out a car and by deftly and gently manoeuvering the controls he kept it framed by my side window, as we followed its innocent and unsuspecting progress through the streets. Kev made it look easy but the Gazelle, while it is a delightful machine to fly, has no automatic stabilisation or autopilot facility; this was pure flying skill.

A small dot could be seen coming from the direction of Lisburn, with its nose light on for easy identification – it was Gazelle 3 crewed by Captain Steve Pengilly and WO1 Ed Doyle, the 2IC and SSM. Careful handling of both helicopters brought XX370 into position for photography, framed by the backdrop of Samson and Goliath, Harland and Wolff's world famous yellow cranes.

Once more, it had been a fascinating afternoon, in the hands of another highly professional aviator.

665 Squadron Gazelle XX370 with Captain Steve Pengilly and WO1 Ed Doyle over Belfast on 24 July 2001, as seen from 665 Gazelle XZ339. Directly below the aircraft can be seen the cranes of the Harland and Wolff shipyard while to the left of the picture the Troon and Stranraer ferries can be identified.

Guy Warner

Royal Flying Corps	Glider Pilot Regiment	Army Air Corps	RAF Station Aldergrove
655 Squadron AAC	665 Squadron AAC	Corps of Royal Electrical and Mechanical Engineers	5 Regiment AAC

The Guidon presented to the Corps in 1994.

5 Regt AAC

111

Bibliography

Newspapers and magazines

Army Air Corps Journal – articles by Staff Sergeant BC Gluning RA, 661 Squadron, Major WP Duthoit, Staffords, Colonel SMW Hickey AAC, Colonel John Goodsir AAC, Major TM Deane AAC, Colonel John Moss AAC, David Michael, TW Pearse, a Royal Military Policewoman, Major R StJ Whidborne AAC, Lieutenant Colonel DJ Ralls DFC, AAC, Captain JR Cross AAC, Brigadier WJ Reed, Lieutenant Colonel AD Fitzgerald MBE, RCT, Brigadier RA Norman-Walker OBE, MC, John Waddy, 657 Squadron, 658 Squadron, 660 Squadron.

Army Air Corps Newsletter – poem by Sergeant H Gater-Smith AAC, article by Captain JM Thwaites AAC

Unpublished manuscript by Major General Sir Peter Downward

REME Magazine September 1958

Visor – Northern Ireland Service News

Belfast Evening Telegraph Tuesday 2 September 1913

Northern Whig Saturday 6 September 1913

Squadron Newsletters and magazines

Cross and Cockade Vol.23 No 4 1992, article by Marvin L Skelton, Capt Dawes and 2 Sqn RFC prepare for war.

Air Pictorial May 1962, articles by Paul Greenhayes, The Origins of the RFC and JM Bruce, The RFC its squadrons and aircraft.

Air Pictorial May 1987 article by JM Bruce, The Birth of British Military Aviation

Air Pictorial September 1962 article by Paul Greenhayes, The Army Air Corps

Air Pictorial February 1970, article by Pete Brown, Treble-Six Squadron.

Air-Britain Digest Summer 1970, article by Mike Draper

The Times 7 September 2002, article by Michael Tillotson.

Daily Telegraph December 2003, obituary of Captain Ian Shoebridge

Ulster Airmail – the Journal of the Ulster Aviation Society

The Scottish Horse 1900–1956 by Lt Col.RMT Campbell-Preston OBE, MC, TD

Regimental, Squadron and Flight scrapbooks.

Archive material supplied by Mr Graham Day, Air Historical Branch (RAF), Ministry of Defence

Books

Farrar-Hockley, General Sir Anthony, *The Army in the Air*, Alan Sutton Publishing Ltd, Stroud, 1994

Kimbell, Alex, *Think Like a Bird*, Airlife Publishing Ltd, Shrewsbury, 2000

Craftsmen of the Army Vols 1 and 2, Corps of the Royal Electrical and Mechanical Engineers, Arborfield, 1970 and 1996

Jefford, Wing Commander CG MBE, RAF, *RAF Squadrons*, Airlife Publishing Ltd, Shrewsbury, 1988

Conyers Nesbit, Roy, *The RAF in Camera 1903–1939*, Sutton, Stroud, 1995

Robertson, Bruce, *The Army and Aviation*, Robert Hale Ltd., London 1981

Dowling, Wing Commander JR MBE, DFC, AFC, *RAF Helicopters – The First Twenty Years*, MOD Air Historical Branch, London, 1987

Barzilay, David, *The British Army in Ulster (Volumes 1–4)*, Century Books, Belfast, 1973–81

Longyard, William H, *Who's Who in Aviation History*, Airlife Publishing Ltd., Shrewsbury, 1994

Burge, Squadron Leader CG OBE, *Complete Book of Aviation*, Pitman & Sons Ltd, London, 1935

McCarron, Donal, *A View from Above – 200 Years of Aviation in Ireland*, The O'Brien Press, Dublin, 2000

Dallas Brett, R, *History of British Aviation 1908–1914*, John Hamilton Ltd, London, 1933

Bruce, JM, *Britain's First Warplanes*, Arms and Armour Press, Poole, 1987

Hayes, KE, *A History of the RAF and USNAS in Ireland 1913–1923*, Irish Air Letter, Dublin, 1988

McCudden, Major James VC, *Five Years in the Royal Flying Corps*, Wren's Park Publishing, Barton-under-Needwood, 2000

Connon, Peter, *In the Shadow of the Eagle's Wings – Aviation in Cumbria 1825–1914*, St Patrick's Press, Penrith, 1982

Lloyd, Mark, *Helicopter Facts and Feats*, Guinness Publishing Ltd., Enfield, 1993

Catchpole, Brian, *The Korean War*, Robinson, London, 2001